The Future Executive

The Future Executive

by Harlan Cleveland

A GUIDE FOR TOMORROW'S MANAGERS

Harper & Row, Publishers

New York · Evanston · San Francisco · London

JUL 25 '73

For Alan

Contents

Preface

For half a lifetime as a public executive, I have wrestled with complexity in public and private employ, in Europe and Asia as well as in the United States. That this experience must have produced some useful ideas about executive leadership is this book's presumption, in both senses of the word.

A career as an executive is not something you plan for yourself. It's the series of accidental changes of job and shifts of scenery on which you look back later, weaving through the story retroactively some thread of logic that was not visible at the time. If you try too carefully to plan your life, the danger is that you will succeed—succeed in narrowing your options, closing off avenues of adventure that cannot now be imagined, perhaps because they are not yet technologically possible. When a student asks me for career advice, I can only suggest that he or she opt for the most exciting "next step" without worrying where it will lead, and then work hard on the job in hand, not pine for the one in the bush. When your job no longer demands of you more than you have, go and do something else. Always take by preference the job you *don't* know

how to do. If you build into your life enough variety of experience, you will be training for leadership, in the role I have
called the Public Executive.

This book is addressed to those who are, or wish to become,
executive leaders in the realm of public responsibility—which
includes not only those who work in "the government" but
also a great many executives in private business, nonprofit
organizations, and the professions. Others can listen in if they
will, but it is the self-conscious executives who most need to
think about their role, because they seem to be inheriting the
earth—though not because they are meek. It is not a comfortable moment to inherit the earth, just when our globe is
revealed as polluted, overpopulated, and in mortal peril from
Man's civilizing intervention in Nature. But it is just these
cosmic dangers which are causing people to turn to those men
and women who see their task in life as bringing people together in organizations to make something different happen.

In this book I suggest that the Public Executives will soon
number one million in the United States alone. Do we have a
profession, those of us who lead by trying to get things done?
What makes us think that taking thought, describing reality,
and spinning theories will improve our performance on the
job? How important is it, anyway, for the executive to know—
rather than just to feel—what he is doing and why?

The classical professions were endowed with a special status
because they dealt with that which determined life and death.
Law and medicine, the military and the ministry, have this in
common. When people realize that they are dependent on a
few for some function, they want those upon whom they depend to be obviously and certifiedly special. But the Public
Executive usually graduates through some specialty; he carries
no license to administer the destiny of others. He need have

no knowledge of a mystery like the men of the cloth, and he cannot impress the public with the special words and hieroglyphs that lawyers and doctors get to use. Nor is the professionalism of administration a specialized and repeatable technique like musketry or cannon-making. Half a century ago, in the high fashion of scientific management, it may have seemed so. But we know now that efficiency has a built-in tendency to take us rapidly to where we will not want to be when we get there. We know this instinctively as we sniff the thickening air, stall in the urban congestion, and count the dead that were killed by systems analysis.

The profession of administration took its rise from concepts in engineering and mechanistic psychology. In this century much of its power came from reform movements that sought to limit bossism and corruption by taking government out of politics and putting more business into government. But the separation between getting-it-decided and getting-it-done could not last. Now the Public Executives don't just implement; they initiate. They don't just carry out the laws; they write most of them. They don't just advise; they act. Just when industrial society's sense of direction is cast loose from "growth" as its mooring, just when "policy" seems elusive and fogbound, just when the other sciences have run amuck, we find the policy sciences in the ill-prepared and hesitant hands of the Public Executives.

A person who has never managed on his own some form of organized cooperation probably cannot be taught what public responsibility is like, in a classroom or elsewhere. The best of the university graduate programs in business management and public administration insist on an internship experience at the tenderest possible age. Formal education for executive responsibility is mostly, and properly, offered for men and women in mid-career who are graduating up one of the ladders to leadership from specialist to general executive. The best arrangement is to catch them just when they are beginning to feel like a lover of realistic art who has wandered by mistake into a gallery of abstract paintings.

Even the formal mid-career training course can be but a small part of an executive's education. Most of it takes place in action. Every executive is a teacher: a good part of his time and effort is devoted to sharing with his more specialized colleagues his own perception of the process in which they are engaged together. For cooperation is the conscious interaction among specialists, and those who understand most deeply what the others are doing, and why, are likely to do their own job best.

I have tried in this book to capture and record the essence of what I have learned in action, so that it can be used by those who choose self-fulfillment by bringing people together in organizations to make something different happen. What emboldens me to write it down is the observation that much of what has proved most valuable in education for leadership is the work of reflective practitioners. One of the earliest books about how to interview, hire, and supervise people was written by a Public Executive who served local princes in China seventeen hundred years ago. Of the codified insights which serve Americans today as general theory in public administration, some of the most durable seem to be the legacy of men of action with a taste for teaching, from Confucius and Kautilya and Julius Caesar and Thomas Aquinas through Machiavelli and Clausewitz and Madison to Woodrow Wilson and Churchill and Barnard and Brownlow and Appleby.

Whatever the publisher's blurb may imply, nobody writes a book like this all at once in a fit of winter ennui or summer inspiration. In one sense it has been developed over a couple of decades. Some phrases and concepts have seen a print shop before, but they have never before dwelt together, taking each other fully into account. I am grateful to the publishers of the *Saturday Review,* the *Annals of the American Academy of Political and Social Science, Public Administration Review,* and the Honolulu *Advertiser* for their tolerance in letting me draw on material which originally appeared in their pages. I have also, with permission, adapted and revised portions of my introductory essay for *Ethics and Bigness,* a volume jointly edited with Harold D. Lasswell and published in 1962 by Harper & Brothers for the Conference on Science, Philosophy and Religion.

Many of my observations, perhaps most, parallel what other executives have felt and scholars of society have written. The erudition to cross-reference my insights with those of others is beyond my ability or ambition. This is my personal statement. If it reinforces or coincides with the statements of others who have seen or studied the processes by which people work together, I am content to leave that discovery to my academic colleagues. If what I have to say cuts across the accepted sociological wisdom—as it does, I think, in guessing that modern technologies will diffuse rather than concentrate leadership in industrial society—I can only explain that I am inclined to trust what I see happening over what I read might happen.

An earlier attempt to write this book was encouraged and assisted by an award from the Fund for Adult Education under its program of Education for Public Responsibility. That effort was suspended when I was invited to leave an academic campus and join the Kennedy Administration; the hiatus lasted almost a decade. Returning to the project after two books on foreign policy, I was fascinated to observe how growing complexity and accelerating change had made earlier formulations obsolete. So this time I decided to focus on the future executive, deriving from an analysis of his probable environment some guesses about what kinds of people, with what kinds of purposes, the organization systems of the future will elevate to executive leadership.

Most of *The Future Executive* was written during the early summer of 1971, at the Villa Serbelloni in Bellagio on Lake Como, in Northern Italy—courtesy of the Rockefeller Foundation. The remainder was done on weekends a few yards from the beach in Kailua, on the Island of Oahu in the State of Hawaii, which made the work as pleasant as hard work can ever be. In the final throes I was greatly assisted by the critical comments of Stephen K. Bailey of Syracuse University and a number of colleagues at the University of Hawaii— Stuart Gerry Brown, Stuart M. Brown, Jr., Henry Kariel, Hahn-Been Lee, Werner Levi, Charles Neff, Glenn Paige, William W. Parsons, Fred Riggs, and Richard Takasaki. The careful and imaginative editing of Douglas R. Price, and the accurate transcriptions and corrections of Betty Tokioka and Doreen Kodama, converted a manuscript into a book. For the notions collected in these pages, I take a somewhat diffident responsibility, knowing how much they are derived from the hundreds of Public Executives I have watched in action.

HARLAN CLEVELAND

Honolulu, Hawaii
October 31, 1971

Of a good leader, who talks little,
When his work is done, his task fulfilled,
They will all say, "We did this ourselves."

—Lao-tse

Part One

Conditions

Chapter 1

Bright Future for Complexity

Things are in the saddle,
And ride mankind.

—*Ralph Waldo Emerson*

People who have not tasted executive responsibility more readily imagine the pains than the joys of sitting where the buck stops. When I worked as an Assistant Secretary of State in Washington, visitors to my office would often say, "I certainly don't envy you," or, "I wouldn't have your job for anything," or something of the sort. The same thing happens with disconcerting frequency to a university president. Perhaps it is part of our egalitarian ethic to believe that those in each organization who draw the most pay and occupy the largest offices are the least happy in their work.

The attraction of responsibility is the sense of relevance that comes from being where the action is. I can best convey my meaning by describing five minutes out of my years as a Public Executive in Washington. These five minutes are admittedly not typical of life in the Federal bureaucracy, but it is fair to say that something almost as gripping happened about once a month and sometimes oftener.

The time was October 23, 1962, at 4:45 of a Tuesday afternoon. I was in my State Department office, watching a television screen as Adlai Stevenson, the U.S. Ambassador to the United Nations, read to the UN Security Council in New York a speech I had helped write, denouncing the presence in Cuba of Soviet nuclear missiles. The telephone rang, and President Kennedy asked a question.

Seven days before, photographs taken by an American U-2 plane had revealed that Soviet missiles had been brought into Cuba, and were nearly ready for operation. Even though the Soviets already had intercontinental ballistic missiles aimed at the United States from Russian silos, planting offensive weapons in our Caribbean back yard was an affront which no U.S. President could let pass.

In urgent secret meetings, an elaborate "scenario" was drafted for getting those missiles out of there. A first tier of some two dozen officials was let in on the secret, and set to work on strategy; a second tier of staff, including myself, was then brought in to flesh out the "scenario" with action papers. Adopting the principle that nonviolence should be tried before either bombing the missile sites or invading Cuba, President Kennedy and his advisers decided to try diplomacy and defensive military action first. Thus on Monday evening the twenty-second, the President revealed the missiles in a nation-wide television speech, calling for a "naval quarantine" of Cuba by the whole Western Hemisphere, and action by the

UN Security Council to persuade Nikita Khrushchev, the head of the Soviet Government, to remove the missiles forthwith. While the President was speaking, we delivered formal calls for an emergency meeting of the Organization of American States in Washington on Tuesday morning, and an emergency meeting of the Security Council in New York at 4 P.M. that afternoon. The idea was to get our Latin-American allies to join in sponsoring the blockade (U.S. naval vessels were already speeding to their positions), and then announce the action as a *collective* security measure when we lodged our formal complaint in the Security Council a few hours later.

Over the weekend Tom Wilson in my office and Arthur Schlesinger from the White House had finished work on Adlai Stevenson's opening speech to the Security Council. I stayed in Washington to backstop the UN part of the scenario. We assumed the OAS action could be completed during Tuesday morning, but several Latin-American ambassadors wanted to get further instructions from their governments during an extended lunch hour. Thus it was that the OAS meeting was only just reconvening over in the Pan American Building when the UN Security Council began its meeting and its President, who was ironically the Soviet representative that month, called on Ambassador Stevenson as the first speaker.

It was still crucial to our plan to present our naval blockade as the product of hemispheric outrage. The State Department's Latin-American chief, Assistant Secretary Edwin Martin, was helping Secretary of State Dean Rusk at the OAS meeting, so I arranged for him to phone me just as soon as the OAS had taken its vote.

The Stevenson speech was being carried on national TV; my then deputy Joseph J. Sisco was in New York to help, and we could see him on television, sitting right behind the UN

Ambassador. Stevenson was reading his speech, and I was following the script on my desk as he spoke. Fifteen minutes from the end of the text, I still had no word from the OAS meeting. Then about 4:40 P.M., Ed Martin called from the Pan American Building to say that all but Uruguay had agreed, and the Secretary authorized us to insert this news in the Stevenson speech.

I called Sisco out of the Security Council meeting, to a little room with a telephone which the U.S. delegation was occupying for just such an emergency. On our Washington television screen we could see Joe Sisco tapped on the shoulder, and hurry off the screen to take my call. I dictated a paragraph to insert in the Stevenson text, and suggested at what point to insert it. Still watching the screen, I saw Sisco come back into view and lay a white sheet of paper on the rostrum.

The Ambassador, however, was in full rhetorical flight. Holding his manuscript off the desk with both hands, he did not appear to notice the precious addition to his speech. I watched with a sinking feeling as he swept on past the point at which I had suggested it should be inserted. Only a minute or two of text remained; there might not be enough time left for another call to New York.

At this point, the phone rang and my secretary, Tess Beach, normally calm and collected, rushed in to report, "The President is on the phone—I mean *personally!*" I reached for the phone, still watching my corner of the Cuba missile scenario come loose in New York. "I've just heard about the OAS action," the President said, speaking even more rapidly than usual. "Is there some way we can get it into Stevenson's speech before he finishes?"

For a giddy instant I wondered what I would have said if we had not thought to cover that base. "We've done an insert on that, Mr. President, and it's just been placed in front of him," I said. "But frankly, I'm not sure he saw it, because—" At that moment, Stevenson reached for the little rectangle of white paper, took it in at a glance, and cleared his throat. Before I could say anything more, President Kennedy, who was naturally watching the same television show in his White House office, cut in. "Oh, I see. He's picking it up and reading it now. Thanks very much, Harlan."

The Cuba missile crisis was not yet over. But mine was.

Executives are people who bring people together in organizations to make something happen. They live and work in the midst of events they help create. And the name of their game is complexity.

"I predict a bright future for complexity in the United States of America," said an E. B. White character in a *New Yorker* story forty-five years ago. ". . . Have you ever considered how complicated things can get, what with one thing always leading to another?"

In the industrialized, "modernized," "developed" nations which rim the Atlantic and Pacific oceans, there is now a pervasive sense of crisis, a vague but deeply felt conviction that something is radically wrong, an irreversible complexity that is bigger than man and may be permanently beyond his control. The young especially are impressed with the illusory and ironic results of the Age of Reason, and are exercising their traditional right to declare the emperor unclothed.

In the summer of 1971 a serious "jury" of American humanists heard adversary arguments and then declared the uses and applications of technology—"a clutch of tools and techniques that gave us the aerosol can, the disposable baby bottle, better health, leisure, human data banks, opinion polls, moonwalks, pellet anti-personnel bombs, the split-level nucleus and other things"—guilty of having, on balance, lowered the quality of human life. Technology and big organizations are by common acclaim the villains of the piece; they are easier targets than man's own addictions to smoking, tin cans, advertising, personalized transportation, and novel gadgetry.

Each generation sees itself at a crucial moment in time, but I think it is now arguable that we are entering one of the great transitions in mankind's history. Behind us is a spectacular success in achieving power over our environment. We not only adjusted to Nature, contriving as all animals do to use it for nourishment and camouflage. We did not merely learn to preserve what was already there. By seeking facts and harnessing energy and bending metal and organizing people, we produced consciously directed change.

The aim was to dominate physical nature by understanding it, to make the environment a product of man's will. As man used reason to break his "natural" shackles, he even began to change himself by blaming his shackles on his own ignorance—a correctible failing—rather than on invisible spirits, overriding principles, or hostile groups of human beings. More power over the environment came to be associated with freedom—if not for all or most, at least for more and more of the few. Certainly in the more "developed" societies, a high proportion of the population makes a wider range of personal choices (where to live, what to do, what to get excited about) than at any previous time. Yet it is now widely doubted that further mastery of our physical environment will produce more freedom for more people.

What brought us to this watershed in human affairs is a sudden enlargement of our ability to organize on a large scale the processes by which one thing leads to another—our capacity, that is, to manage complexity. But we have concentrated this talent on the control of physical "progress"; the complexity crisis has been produced by our loss of control over its human consequences. Man is bright enough to invent the internal combustion engine, burn off garbage in the open air, and build sewers to get waste out of his own home; but one thing leads to another, and a baffling condition of air and water pollution results. Organized medicine succeeds in lengthening life and reducing infant mortality, and creating a "population problem." Agricultural science makes it possible to give every man, woman, and child a decent diet; controversy then breaks out over our evident failure to do just that. The science and mathematics of meteorology improve weather forecasting, which everybody likes. But they also will make it possible to change the world's weather at human command—and we have not even begun to think hard about the ethics of using *that* power. Modern psychology sweeps away the myths that misled but comforted our forebears—but still gropes for something to put in their place. Modern management develops ways of organizing large numbers of people in loose organizations that successfully perform highly complex operations—and produces an epidemic of frustration about bureaucracy, even generates a revolt against bigness as such.

Benjamin Franklin, even while advertising the potentials of technology, perceived the threat of the 1970s and beyond. "The rapid progress *true* science now makes," he wrote in a letter to Joseph Priestley, "occasions my regretting sometimes that I was born so soon. It is impossible to imagine the height to which may be carried, in a thousand years, the power of man over matter. We may perhaps learn to deprive large masses of their gravity . . . for the sake of easy transport. Agriculture may diminish its labour and double its produce;

all diseases may by sure means be prevented or cured, not excepting even that of old age. . . . O that moral science were in a fair way of improvement, that men would cease to be wolves to one another, and that human beings would at length learn what they now improperly call humanity." Much of the technological change Franklin thought might take a thousand years has come about in a couple of hundred. But we have not yet ceased to be wolves to one another. The interlocked discriminations of race and poverty, and the brutalizing influence of war, bear witness.

"Officer," says a woman arrested for driving the wrong way on a one-way street, "has it occurred to you that the arrow may be pointing in the wrong direction?" She is speaking for us all.

The social fallout of science requires an enormous range of new kinds of decisions to be made by somebody from day to day. Some of them are directly the result of scientific invention and technological innovation; other new decisions are the consequence of the human congestion that science makes possible.

My grandfather did not regard himself as responsible for racial oppression, or international relations, or the plight of the cities, or other gaps in the "moral science" of his day. He did not need to have an opinion on legalized abortion, let alone on whether scientists ought to reach into people's molecules to induce mutations in their genes. Grandfather read Jules Verne and doubtless assumed that man would one day reach the Moon, but (though he was a lawyer and a politician) he did not think hard about creating law for outer space and celestial bodies. Nor did he worry about the testing and control of nuclear weapons, or brood about insurance against nuclear accidents. It did not even trouble his conscience to spray his garden with pest-killers; their use was neither widespread nor efficient.

Now we are quite suddenly in the presence of machines and drugs and procedures that can change the balance of nature, ruin the human environment, activate or tranquilize a teenager, alter human personality, raise or lower intelligence, enhance or impair memory and learning, make births more various or uniform, and extend the very frontiers of death. Machines are taking over most of the work that "unskilled workers" used to do; new weaponry has altered the arithmetic of war and the strategies of peace; new means of transport and communications make individuals more independent and cultures and societies more interdependent. Before the scientific revolution in farming and medicine, there was not effectively a "world food problem" or a "world health problem"; there was merely an unavoidable prevalence of starvation and disease. Now that something can be done about these ancient afflictions, decisions have to be made by somebody to do or not to do that something.

The new decisions do not seem to be a substitute for the older kinds of decisions—they are net additions to the quantum of public responsibility. Nor are they just the business of "responsible officials": every man and woman takes on more responsibility as the margins for social error dwindle. A hundred years ago North Americans were scattered about on farms or in rural towns with room to spare. Now that two-thirds of us live in or near cities, our accountability to each other is incalculably greater. Youthful activities which used to be tolerated in rural societies are regarded in cities as deviant behavior; high-spirited youth may not have changed as much as have the norms against which juvenile conduct is measured.

11

Driving a Buick on a crowded freeway requires more continuous exercise of a sense of responsibility to others than driving a Model T on a rural byway. The pilot of an airliner has to make more split-second decisions, is responsible for more lives, and is more dependent on the judgment of controllers at his destination, than the man who drove the stagecoach. If a man wanted to shoot up his neighbor in the Kentucky mountains, the other residents could avoid participation in the feud, which might smolder for generations as a limited war between two families. A similar feud will not be tolerated by urban society. The interrelatedness of everything puts society's conscience in the hands of the innocent bystander.

The effect of technological change on the character of human decisions is illustrated with almost too much drama in the rapid mutation in air and missile defense. It was hard enough to get used to the idea that our personal safety might depend on a small group of young men watching for enemy invasion at an outpost of the Distant Early Warning Line. As new technologies shortened the warning times, responsibility for being right the first time was more and more diffused to the far corners of the earth, where a sleepy GI could cost us precious minutes, or an overzealous one cost us the future itself. Newer technologies were then devised to reserve to the President the kinds of decisions that used to be made by subordinate commanders—decisions about the movement of troops or the firing of long-range weapons—even if there were only a few moments to decide and the President were on the golf course or at a dinner party. But the more computerized the technology becomes and the shorter the time-span for the last-minute application of human judgment, the more fanciful becomes the notion that the President is still in tactical charge.

In an antiballistic missile system, for example, experts have

12

to program into computers the possible characteristics of incoming missiles, so the machine can identify, track, and fire at them before they get to their targets, a matter of minutes after they appear over the horizon. The decision to fire is no longer, in such a system, the Commander in Chief's; that decision has been predelegated, with instructions, to the computer. The President's responsibility is exercised, if at all, much earlier in the process, by trying to make sure the experts who programmed the computer knew what they were doing. And how does he make sure of that?

The extraordinary growth in the number and public importance of decisions to be made will require new kinds of organizations, managed in new ways by new kinds of people. Here, in sum, is my argument:

The organizations that get things done will no longer be hierarchical pyramids with most of the real control at the top. They will be *systems*—interlaced webs of tension in which control is loose, power diffused, and centers of decision plural. "Decision-making" will become an increasingly intricate process of multilateral brokerage both inside and outside the organization which thinks it has the responsibility for making, or at least announcing, the decision. Because organizations will be more horizontal, the way they are governed is likely to be more collegial, consensual, and consultative. The bigger the problems to be tackled, the more real power is diffused and the larger the number of persons who can exercise it—if they work at it. This trend is visible in totalitarian as well as democratic societies. "Collective leadership" and committee work are not conclusive evidence of democratic feelings. They are imperatives of bigness and complexity.

Bigness and complexity are also blurring the traditional line between "public" and "private." The managers of "private" enterprise, profit or nonprofit, will move further toward the concept that they are responsible to people-in-general, and thereby bring the government more into their affairs. At the same time the government will farm out to the "private sector" a growing proportion of the public business. No large organization, whatever its formal ownership, will be able to escape its public responsibility.

They will be manned, these new-style public-private horizontal systems, by a new breed of men and (increasingly) women. I call them the Public Executives, people who manage public responsibilities whether in "public" or "private" organizations. They will climb ladders of specialized achievement, into positions that require them to "get it all together." Their administrative style will have to be adjusted to an environment which is ill described by drawing square and static diagrams on two-dimensional charts; it will feel more like a continuous chemical reaction in a liquefied solution. The Public Executives will enjoy complexity—or look for some less demanding line of work.

If what is wrong with modern society is the weakness of "moral science," as Franklin foresaw, Public Executives will carry the main responsibility for mixing values with technology. In a society built more and more on lateral relationships, it is already time to revise Paul Appleby's famous definition of "policy," which applied so well to a hierarchical culture. For Appleby, policy was the decisions that are made at your level and higher. But for the Public Executive of the future, policy will be mostly his or her own sense of direction, modified by negotiation with his or her peers.

It is too easy to describe the future executives as "change agents"—accelerating change is their destiny, and like it or not they will be its agents. It will not be a comfortable role. Picking their way through the jungle of complexity and making up their own policy as they go along, Public Executives will have every reason to feel sorry for themselves. But they will also apprehend that the function of the executive is to make the difficult choices others are reluctant to make. And in any society those who choose the most have the most reason to feel free.

Chapter 2

A Web of Tensions

A man is a bundle of relations, a knot of roots, whose flower and fruitage is the world.
—*Ralph Waldo Emerson*

Sermons, subway posters, and popular psychology have conditioned us to think of human cooperation as ideally pacific, relaxing, untense. The future executive will know better. His professional destiny is not a tangle of togetherness but a web of tensions.

When you work as part of a large organization, you are bound to sense what the philosophers of administration find so troublesome to describe—that an organization consists not merely of the people in it, but of something more abstract: the interaction of these people with each other. Even if you know personally all the people in an organization, you still know very little about it until you learn how they work to-

16

gether, what cross-purposes and multiple aims are served by their competition and cooperation with each other. You also observe that each individual allocates to any one organization only a fractional part of his energy, loyalty, and time.

These two perceptions lead some executives to think that the primary task of any organization is to get its members to cooperate with it. This is the line that Chester Barnard took in his landmark book of administrative theory, *The Functions of the Executive*. The main problem of administration, according to this view, is to get members of the agency's own staff to allocate to it an adequate fraction of their loyalty, and to get clients or constituents or customers to cooperate in the appropriate ways, buying the organization's products or services, paying its taxes or prices, accepting its regulation of their behavior, and participating in the processes through which the organization makes up its "mind."

Certainly every agency has to get its staff and its constituents to cooperate. But in a modern large-scale organization, getting people to cooperate is too easy; and it is by no means the most pressing problem. The manager of an administrative process can always elicit cooperation by not reaching the real issues that divide people from each other, or by diverting attention from fundamental where-are-we-going-anyway questions. Many errors of judgment can be traced to too much consensus too early in the game.

During the Eisenhower Administration there were complaints that Sherman Adams, who managed the White House staff, systematically prevented disagreements from reaching the President. The technique was described to me by a participant at the time: Sensing a disagreement between two Cabinet members, Adams would persuade them not to raise the subject with the President in the Cabinet meeting but instead to meet with Adams afterward. After the first ten minutes of the private meeting, it would become clear that the two officials were diametrically opposed to each other on a basic issue of public policy. Adams would then suggest going through the policy paper paragraph by paragraph. Even the most acrimonious disagreement can be effectively buried if enough double-meaning words are used; every foreign office employs skilled practitioners of fuzziness for this purpose. (". . . One can always get an agreed paper by increasing the vagueness and generality of its statements," said Dean Acheson. "The staff of any interdepartmental committee has a fatal weakness for this kind of agreement by exhaustion.") Adams and the Cabinet members would then go in to President Eisenhower, who would inquire whether there was agreement—which there was, on the paper if not on the buried issue. Pleased at these signs of cooperation within his Administration and completed staff work by his assistant, the President would then approve the paper, leaving the policy untouched.

Cooperation by reticence led the Kennedy Administration into its worst mistake, the Bay of Pigs affair. The President, inheriting a Central Intelligence Agency plan for the clandestine invasion of Cuba, assumed that the Joint Chiefs of Staff would speak up if they did not think these military plans would work; the Joint Chiefs, according to one of them, were awed by the bright new political hero in the White House, and "thought they should speak when spoken to." In fact, of course, they spoke a good deal, but some of the crucial uncertainties were never surfaced; cooperation was excellent in the sense that argument was avoided. The CIA's operation went forward—to an immediate and embarrassing debacle.

The dangers of too little tension were all too clearly illustrated by the way President Lyndon Johnson escalated the war in Vietnam. The Pentagon Papers of 1971, and some of the President's own writings, have confirmed what was obvious even at the time: that by the spring of 1965 the President had narrowed the circle of trusted advisers on Vietnam to less than a dozen men, only one of whom did not believe the North Vietnamese could be brought to a sensible bargain by bombing their villages and fighting them with American ground troops. The staff work supporting each escalatory step, read in the illumination of hindsight, seems designed to find arguments for more bombing and a U.S. combat role, on the assumption (which turned out after some hesitations to be correct) that the President intended to turn up the heat until the men in Hanoi were ready to talk peace.

LBJ's mentor and former idol, President Franklin Roosevelt, encouraged disputations about policy, frequently inviting uninvolved citizens to lunch to add to his perspective on the public issues of the day. President Johnson's growing reluctance to subject his Vietnam policy to wide consultation, with Americans or allies, led the nation into a major strategic error.

During this period and later, the President encouraged George Ball, the Under Secretary of State, to bring forward the arguments for a different policy in Vietnam; some of the resulting memos are in the Pentagon Papers. This narrow channel of internal dissent may have helped the President persuade himself that he was taking all points of view into account, but he was publicly unimpressed and privately intolerant of opinions contrary to the direction in which his own instincts were taking him. His relations with the Senate leadership, which once made him so effective a Majority Leader, deteriorated to formal information sessions that could not be called "consultation." By early 1968 the President's sense of isolation from many of the Senate's Democrats was an acute personal embarrassment to him.

I was briefly a witness to the President's agony. At the end of February 1968, I was on a visit to Washington from my post as Ambassador to NATO. After a meeting in the White House Oval Room, the President asked me to stay on in Washington and visit with some of the liberal Senators on his behalf.

"I'm out of touch with those fellows," said the Senate's former leader, "and I don't have anybody who can talk with them. Adlai [Stevenson] is dead, and ol' George [Ball] has left me." Since I had previously worked with Stevenson at the UN, the President asked me to visit all the liberal Democrats I could in the Senate, start a conversation with them about NATO, and then listen to what they said about Vietnam. A week later, I sent to the President, through Secretary Rusk, a memo predicting a filibuster by at least fifteen Senators on some issue related to military policy a little later in the Congressional session. You would, I reported, have to go all the way back to 1919–20, to the "little band of willful men" who checkmated Woodrow Wilson on U.S. ratification of the League of Nations Covenant, to find a minority in the Senate as militantly determined as that in March of 1968. I quoted Senator Albert Gore of Tennessee: "We think the chariot is heading for the precipice, and if that's the only way to stop it, we'll take its wheels off." I did not need to tell Lyndon Johnson what damage to the nation's unity and morale could be done by the long and divisive constitutional struggle which a dozen or more Senators could readily provoke if they used with determination the permissive parliamentary rules of the United States Senate.

Four weeks later the President stopped the bombing and announced he would not run for re-election. I have no reason, except the bureaucrat's normal overestimate of his own relevance, to suppose that my report was a significant factor in that enormous decision. What the incident probably does illustrate is that the President in those critical weeks was deliberately enlarging the circle of consultation—and sharply altered his course as a result.

One lesson is common to each of these stories: too much agreement, from too narrow a group, makes for decisions that don't "work." Wide consultation, on the other hand, teaches the consulter enough about the prospective reaction to a line of action to enable him to modify it.

To complete the bipartisan inventory, take the decision by President Nixon to invade Cambodia in the spring of 1970. On April 20, in a TV roundup on Southeast Asia, the President gave no hint of such a policy; on April 30 the Cambodia raid was begun. Wide consultation was evidently sacrificed to secrecy and speed. The White House, it seems, was genuinely surprised at the violent reaction on the nation's college and university campuses, a number of which closed for the semester's duration. Yet the Cambodia operation was planned for what is traditionally "panty-raid" week on the American college campus. Something was bound to blow that week on hundreds of campuses; the President's timing assured that the something which blew was organized opposition to the Nixon Administration. It now appears that the invasion decision was taken primarily on military advice, and that nobody in tune with the nation's campuses had the President's ear at the time. (The President's diplomatic advisers may have been missing, too: the U.S. neglected to get an invitation from the Cambodian Government before moving in force onto its territory.)

In a word: it is too easy to get people in an organization to cooperate, especially if they are few, and if they share too closely the orientation and interest of the chief executive. The wise executive will take as his major task the reverse of inducing cooperation. He will deliberately induce a degree of tension within the organization, enough loud and cheerful argument among its members so that all possible outcomes are analyzed, the short-term benefits are compared with the long-run costs, the moral dilemmas are illuminated, and the public-relations effects are analytically examined. (As to the latter, it would be hard to improve on Paul Appleby's prescription that an executive should, before acting, make sure he knows the answers to four questions: "Who's going to be mad? How mad? Who's going to be glad? How glad?")

The fruitful friction of administration is to be found in almost any organization that seems to be working effectively toward its goals. The wise Public Executive wants his colleagues to disagree—that is why he puts them in different places, assigns them to defend differing viewpoints, and expects them to "represent" different outside interests in the internal staff debates. General William Reeder, a former Comptroller of the U.S. Army, tells of inspecting a budget unit at an Army base where the colonel in charge told him proudly, "This year, for the first time I can remember, we in the field agree completely with the planning figures we have received from the Pentagon." General Reeder was not pleased. "That makes either you or the man that did the Washington estimate surplus to the Army's needs," he retorted. "Which of you shall we fire?"

There is an almost infallible sign by which to identify the members of large organizations who do not understand the uses of tension. They are the folk who always want the ambiguities "clarified." But in large organization systems the ambiguities are often of the essence. An example is the recur-

22

ring dilemma about whether to get things done by function or by region.

In almost any large system—from IBM in the "private" sector to AID in the "public"—there is a compromise between two principles of organization, one favoring the resolution of problems by geography, the other by subject matter. The foreign-aid agency has to have experts on agriculture, health, population, industrial technology, urban planning, and any other specialized field in which it is purveying assistance to developing nations. It must also have strong country missions, backed up by regional offices at headquarters, to work closely with the developing nations on their over-all development plans. There is a normal natural warfare between these two main elements of the foreign-aid system. Yet nearly every time the aid agency is reorganized, some attempt is made to have one or the other principle of organization "win." The result is a cyclical pattern of reorganization: first the geographical offices have the most influence, then the functional offices get back on top, then the cycle starts all over again. What is important is that neither of the "sides" should "win" the seesaw battle for relevance—they are supposed to be looking at the same moon from different modules. The resulting clash of judgment should be designed to help the administrator and his colleagues to fashion a program that makes sense both in terms, say, of agricultural science and in terms of a nation's development priorities.

The Department of Health, Education, and Welfare is organized in Washington along health-education-welfare lines. But the Secretary of HEW also has regional representatives who try to shepherd into one flock the Regional Commissioner of Social Security, the regional man for the U.S. Office of Education, the regional Public Health Service officer, and the others. International Business Machines has a similar built-in ambiguity. At headquarters (though not all at the same sites) IBM has a Data Processing Group, a World Trade Corporation, some smaller "profit" agencies, together with staff (or "cost") functions. But the company also has to have regional and local branch offices to make sure that all its activities in, say, Kansas or Hawaii make sense in relation to each other and are serving IBM's subjective human purpose (as defined from time to time by its executives).

In either of these cases the only honest answer to the query "Who's *really* in charge around here?" is: "It depends." For some purposes the regional manager may have a decisive voice; on other issues what looks good in one region may be bad corporate policy from a national or international perspective. Nor does the structure determine who is influential on issues in controversy. Careful homework and force of personality count for much, especially in an environment of rapid change such as the computer business or the delivery of health care.

So when you hear someone say he cannot get on with his part of the job until the lines of authority and responsibility are clarified, look sharp to see whether clarity or ambiguity better serves the system's purposes. The complaint may simply be a warning signal that you have a colleague who has not yet found his footing on the web of tensions. And when you hear an associate explaining to his staff the principle of constructive ambiguity, put him down as an executive for the world of tomorrow.

The tensions inside an organization should of course differ from those on the outside in one important way. Their emotional content has to be low. The Public Executive learns to represent his views with vigor, without letting his self-esteem (or his ability to sleep at night) ride on the outcome of each argument about policy, procedure, or jurisdiction. Tension, drained so far as possible of its *personal* content, is what makes modern large-scale organization possible. It is what enables people who have learned to work together inside an organization to play the let's-pretend game of representing for purposes of staff discussion the main outside interests concerned with the organization's decisions, and yet to agree with other executives about what to do next. That would be far more difficult if real representatives of the outside interests were bargaining with each other, without the incentive of a common purpose.

What sets the "developed" off from the "underdeveloped" societies is precisely the presence in the former of much larger numbers of people capable of performing a designated function as part of a large-scale system, dovetailing their emotional commitments with the organization's purposes. (Both personal commitments and institutional objectives are usually modified in the process.) A "developed" society requires of each executive that he act in each office he holds more or less the way it is functional for a person in that position to act. He must be able to deal with other executives in the system not merely as himself but as a function. He must be able to argue forcefully for his policy preferences, yet not "take it personally" when they do not prevail. In a developed industrial culture, an executive may come to his task from Texas politics, a Los Angeles ghetto, a Chicago trade union, or a Proper Bostonian tribe, but he finds ways of marrying his heritage, training, and personality to some concept of what is required of a person doing the job he is supposed to do as the deputy assistant director of this or that. In the more personalized cultures of the less developed lands, the executive's family or clique or tribe or individual *amour-propre* tends to override his functions, with damage to the system that mounts as complexity increases. A major purpose of education in the developing nations these days is to grow people with a vocation for organizationally relevant behavior.

Of course we know now that behaving the way *somebody else thinks* the deputy assistant director should behave is not good enough; we have come to a time when, as Churchill wrote of the moments before a Great War, "each person had only to do his duty to wreck the world." Along with managing the tension system, the future executive will be more and more responsible for figuring out where the whole system should be going, and trying to make sure by various forms of personal commitment (up to and including resignation) that it is going there. The resulting traumas and opportunities are discussed in Chapters 8 and 9.

An organization, then, is the relations among its participants. Those relations, like a man's muscles, work best under tension. When you see an organization without tension, it is like watching a drunk—the muscles are flaccid, the coordination is poor, the behavior is erratic, and the "bundle of relations" is in danger of falling on its face.

As long as most of mankind's social tasks could be accomplished inside single hierarchical pyramids, it was convenient enough to call such structures "organizations." But more and more important social tasks in an industrialized society can only be accomplished by linking together a congeries of organizations, each contributing its part to some larger purpose which is presumed to be shared by them all. The future-oriented word for "organization" is "system."

If an organization is the relations among its members, an

organization system is "a bundle of relations." The technical use of the now popular term "system" includes complexities which man cannot manage (the solar system), or man is just beginning to understand (the nervous system), or are created by man for his own use (a language, a school system, a weapons system). I will use the word "system" to mean a bundle of relations which is (1) aimed at a subjective human purpose and (2) so large and complicated that all the connections among its parts cannot be known by any one person even if that person is said to be "in charge." *

For the past half-century or so, much of what we have called progress has resulted from using systems concepts to analyze problems and organize to solve them. The study of organisms and organizations as systems has provided a tool for break-throughs in a wide variety of fields. With the help of computers, we have discovered more effective ways to organize our thinking about everything from weather forecasting and conflict theory to airplane reservations and getting the paychecks out on time. We can illumine complex systems: structural linguistics, information theory, cybernetics, and information feedback systems; input-output analysis and linear programming (mathematical methods for allocating resources), systematic theories of economic growth, econometrics, cost-benefit analysis, and PPBS (Planning-Programming-Budgeting Systems); game theory, statistical decision theory, survey research (including attitude polling), operations research, and technology assessment. With computer simulation, we can forecast economic processes, estimate environmental impacts, study social events as the interplay of many conditions, construct decision models,

* There are hundreds of ways to use, and define, the word "system." Here I am using the summary definition of Anatol Rapaport in the *International Encyclopedia of the Social Sciences,* refined by John P. Craven in a new book on *Ocean Engineering Systems* (The M.I.T. Press, 1971).

and apply mathematical probability to possible social and political futures.

The practicing executive can have only a general idea of the potential and the limitations of such efforts to think more systematically about where we are going and how to get there. But he is justified in guessing that systematic study and rigorous planning are blunt tools at best. Detailed planning ahead was highly popular for a time. But we have already had too many examples of detailed and systematic plans going in the wrong direction. The McNamara Pentagon laid down men and equipment in Vietnam more efficiently than this had ever been done before in military history—but it turned out that, on reflection, we did not want them to be there. Quantitative methods for measuring pacification of the Vietnam countryside turned out to be public-relations gimmicks at best and instruments of self-delusion at worst. The effort to systemize success or failure in the Vietnam war—in the absence of that old dependable analytical tool, the map with drawn battle lines—led to a high dependence on counting dead bodies; killing thus became the self-justifying "subjective human purpose" of the military system for that time and place, and our wider political aims, not to mention our humanity and our moral purposes, were sidetracked as unsystematic because immeasurable.

Whether plans can be quantified, and progress in pursuing them measured, depends of course on the subjective human purpose which each "bundle of relations" is supposed to accomplish. In some forms of scientific inquiry and some large engineering systems—building a new factory, developing a nuclear sub, getting a man on the Moon—the main components and outcomes can be rather accurately specified, counted, tested, evaluated, and, if necessary, replicated. But in dealing with the assessment of the future results of science and technology, for which more and more Public Executives find themselves responsible, the quantifiable parts of the analysis often turn out to be the less important parts. That is why detailed planning ahead is no longer so much in vogue. The future executive will need a new definition of planning: *improvisation on a general sense of direction.* The irreducible functions of the executive are to define the subjective human purposes, and then make sure that his (or her) part of the system keeps moving toward them.

It is organization systems, combined with systematic scientific inquiry, that have brought mankind to the present heights of progress-cum-frustration. If we are to take hold of our future, we are going to require more comprehensive systems, not simpler ones. As one example, computerized business systems and law-enforcement procedures have already raised large questions about their effect on the individual's right of privacy; the system that creates the new procedures must therefore include the analysis and protection of the rights of individuals. A "system" that invented the internal combustion engine and put it in an automobile was obviously not comprehensive enough; we know to our sorrow (in some cities we literally weep in the smog) that the system planning should have included an assessment of the second- and third-order consequences of mass-producing that new technology. Whether we can do better with nuclear energy, weather modification, laser beams, genetic engineering, and the rest will depend largely on the vision, the ethical perceptions, and the administrative skills of our future executives.

Chapter 3

The Future Is Horizontal

Who shall decide when doctors disagree?
—Alexander Pope

At Parris Island, South Carolina, on April 8, 1956, a Marine
drill instructor named Staff Sergeant Matthew C. McKeon
barked an order to a platoon of recruits, who promptly
marched into water over their heads. Some of them could not
swim, and drowned. A few of them must have reflected on that
possibility ahead of time. Yet published reports of the incident
suggest that none of the recruits seriously considered disobey-
ing the marching order.

That Parris Island platoon can stand as the extreme case of
"vertical administration," in which a maximum of authority
has been "delegated upward" to the issuers of orders by those
who receive them. Somewhere near the other end of the long

and colorful spectrum of human organizations, you will find an academic administrator working with faculty, students, alumni, trustees, legislators, and other citizens concerned with higher education. None of these would walk across the street, let alone into dangerous waters, on orders from an administrator.

Academic administration is probably not the most extreme case at the "horizontal" end of the spectrum. Hospitals are. Members of a university's staff are at least on its payroll. The medical staff of a hospital are on the patients' payroll. The relations between doctors and hospital administrators are typically more arm's-length than those between a college dean and his teaching faculty.

Between Sergeant McKeon's small platoon at one end and a large hospital at the other, it is theoretically possible to line up all kinds of organizations with which the citizen deals, and in which most of us work. Reading from the "vertical" end, we can identify military organizations, family businesses, small denominational colleges, trade unions, courts, philanthropic foundations, journalistic enterprises, large corporations, law firms, government departments, voluntary agencies, scientific laboratories, research houses, larger colleges, universities, medical groups, and hospitals.

Any such listing is incomplete and arbitrary. There are distinctions within each category, between organizations where the style of management is looser and more collegial, and others where recommendations go up and orders come down in traditional hierarchical fashion. But these differences in horizontalness will be less and less important to the future executive, because *every* kind of organization is moving away from vertical administration toward more consultative styles of operation.

The reason is both obvious and fundamental: irrespective of their purpose, modern organizations must be big enough to handle their functions, and that means bigger all the time. Scientific discovery and technological innovation require larger and larger "systems" to contain, channel, and control the new complexities. Growing size in turn is directly correlated with wider dispersion of real power inside each system, and also with more sharing of real responsibility with outsiders. In these circumstances the making of "decisions" cannot be described or understood in the recommendations-up-orders-down language of hierarchical administration. The "devolution" of responsibility goes mostly outward, not downward.

At every level of government the increasing complexity of the subject matter, plus the increasing sensitivity to the interdependence of domains previously accepted as fairly separable, multiplies the number of executives whose special knowledge is essential or whose oxen are gored. In every community, and notably in the metropolitan areas, a new pattern of leadership now spreads the power to affect the community's destiny, breaking the leadership monopolies traditionally held by businessmen, business lawyers, and early-arriving ethnic groups. In the new competition for influence, the ticket of admission for the leaders of any aspiring group is now skill in organization, and a working knowledge of interorganizational complexity. For every new decision—a new hospital, a downtown plaza, a poverty program, a community college, a metropolitan water plan, or whatever—involves the creative management of multiple authorities, "private" as well as public.

As complexity is compounded, executives (the people whose profession is to get things done) must therefore widen the circle of those consulted in making decisions. If a zoning decision is in prospect, neighbors and conservationists must be invited to a public hearing. If education is the topic, parents and teachers and students and administrators—and surrogates for the taxpayers, too—must all be brought into the discussion. If profits are the purpose, they must be shared with employees whose productivity will make or break the balance sheet. It is not enough for a mayor or a governor to announce a tax program; he must produce a credible aggregation of economic experts in its support—and that means asking them what they think before he announces what he thinks. If the President proposes a measure of national defense, it is not enough to say that his Cabinet and Chiefs of Staff are for it; the leading Congressional specialists on the subject, together with a spectrum of citizens ranging from professors to veterans' representatives, must have been visibly asked for their opinion.

This is why top executives, who look from the outside as though they hold so much "power" in their hands, are themselves more impressed with the difficulty of getting anything done—and find themselves spending most of their time in lateral consultations. Executives accustomed to more vertical modes or narrower ranges of responsibility, freshly appointed to top positions in large public-interest organizations, are often surprised at the way their options are narrowed by lateral bargaining and agreements among their subordinates before matters are pushed "up" for their decision. "I do not rule Russia," said Czar Nicholas at a moment of frustration. "Ten thousand clerks do."

My own observation in Washington was that the higher one's rank, the fewer unreviewed decisions one makes. The man who drives the power lawn mower on government property makes a number of unreviewed decisions—where to mow first, how long to leave the grass, when the machine needs servicing. On the kinds of questions which are "policy" for a person whose task is to mow the lawn, he comes close to being his own boss. But at the upper levels of the bureaucracy the executive seldom writes a letter he signs, or signs a letter he writes. He writes for those with wider responsibilities, and those with narrower functions write for him. On matters where he makes the "final decision," he is surrounded—or prudently arranges to surround himself—with an intricate network of lateral clearances, advisory committees, and personal relationships with veto groups and political personalities whose views must be reconciled, offset, or discounted before a decision at that level will "stick."

Within a major organization system like the U.S. Department of State, the requirement for lateral clearance is self-enforcing. An Assistant Secretary of State, as head of one of the baronial bureaus, has plenty of formal authority to send out on behalf of the Secretary of State a message of instruction to ambassadors abroad. But if his cable slices across the jurisdiction of another Assistant Secretary, as is likely to be the case on any matter of real importance, the message had better be cleared even at the cost of delay. If it is not, the other Assistant Secretary has a powerful counterweapon to enforce his rights: during the next few days he can send off without clearance a cable or two that his offending colleague should have seen. Inside a big government department such self-enforcing "honor systems" make for too many lateral clearances. Each person who drafts a policy paper is more than anxious to preserve his right to see and criticize the policy initiatives of others.

I once worked with a very intelligent businessman whose previous experience consisted mostly of running a small newspaper. He was appointed to head the Far Eastern Division of the huge U.S. foreign-aid agency, and promptly started to operate as if he were responsible for all the decisions about U.S. aid to the Far East. The people responsible for agricultural aid, public health aid, technical assistance policy, loan policy, budget policy, and Congressional relations kept complaining to me that the Far Eastern Program director was trying to operate without reference to them, and muttering that they would "show him" by making their own decisions about aid to Asian destinations without checking with him. But not long after he had taken office, I knew that our new colleague would survive the transition from owner-operator of a small business to public servant in a complex international enterprise. He came into my office one evening with the beginning of a smile on his face and said, "I'm director of the Far Eastern Program, but that doesn't mean I direct the Far Eastern Program, does it? I mean I don't make any decisions on my own. I'm really a sort of broker, I guess."

Part of the problem is doubtless with the word "decision." It connotes the end of a finite piece of business called "decision-making." Yet the typical decision in a complex organization system is simply one milestone in a long and highly dynamic trip. The executive, who is by function and temperament in motion, must see each "decision" as the sequel to earlier and the prologue to his later moves—and those of others.

If organization systems are likely to grow in size and complexity, if decisions within and among them will require more and more horizontal consensus, we should find in the most horizontal kinds of organizations some useful clues to the likely forms of future systems. A university, for example, is already well past the age of administrative pyramids. It is a self-conscious, even intentional community; its various parts organize to bargain multilaterally with the others, and all of them (together and sometimes separately) interact with a wider community which supports and criticizes, encourages and limits, the community of scholars and students. The consequent choreography may have predictive value for organization systems in fields remote from higher education.

In skeleton terms, a university community consists of students, faculty, administrators, and trustees or regents. Just outside, looking on and sometimes intervening in university management, is a wider community containing alumni, taxpayers, and their elected representatives. No one is fully in charge. What happens on any given issue is the product of negotiation among these veto groups. The executive, however, has a marginal advantage over the others: he works full time at university governance, unlike the external critics and controllers and also unlike the teachers, the scholars, and the students; he is also an individual with a professional staff, not a committee like the board or faculty senate or student organizations. But he still has to make his peace, laterally, with all of them.

University students are now the subject as well as the object of higher education. Time was that a student, entering an ivied campus in its rural setting, left to his academic mentors substantial control of his curriculum, his life style, and even his attire. The university student is now typically a citizen of an urban campus, and most of the traditional grants of authority to his mentors have been withdrawn. Students are now asserting jurisdiction, within very wide limits, over their own deportment, their own living arrangements, and in some programs (especially the liberal arts) the courses they will take and the style of the teaching. The brighter the student, the more opportunities he or she has to tailor-make a personal curriculum which is different from any other student's. Student organizations supervise most purely student activities, manage student activity centers, and often dispose of very large sums of money derived from student fees.

Students do not and cannot "govern" a university—and

where they seriously try to do so, as in some parts of Latin America, the resulting institutions are more narrowly political than broadly educational in their purposes and outcomes. What students do is organize as constituency pressure groups to make themselves heard on student affairs, the quality of the faculty's teaching, the university's priorities, and national issues. But except for a few "permanent students," especially at the graduate level, neither leaders nor followers stay on campus long enough to sustain a bid for "power" in so complex, expensive, and long-lived an enterprise as a large university. The student population also shifts more than it did a generation ago, since the typical academic career of a university student now features one or more interruptions away from school before a degree is earned.

"Student government" usually takes a legislative form, with representative elections for student senators. But the formal student leaders are often overshadowed by leaders of other student organizations, concerned with political, professional, social, and religious aims. The result is a classic form of pressure-group politics. The students do not regard themselves as "working for" the university and its constitutional governors; rather, they regard themselves as claimants on the university, favored claimants because they are its *raison d'être*. In the event the institution is insufficiently responsive to their interests as they define them, they reserve the right to criticize it, or even to close it down if they can.

Both their attitudes and many of their more activist techniques—the demonstration, the mass visitation, the strike—are familiar in the development of the labor movement, and are increasingly in vogue among client groups off campus. Welfare recipients are asserting their right to monitor welfare policy. Poor people want to help manage the War on Poverty.

Residents in housing projects are intervening directly in public-housing policy. Citizens of a threatened neighborhood no longer have much hesitation in organizing to bargain collectively about the location of a sewage outfall, the routing of a freeway, the pollution from a factory smokestack, the site of a community college, or the placement of a traffic light. "Student power" is hardly more than a step ahead of the wider trend toward "client power."

If university students are to be compared to clients in the off-campus world, the manner in which a university faculty shares in governance may be seen as the forerunner of wider participation by the professional staffs in other kinds of organizations. As machines take over more and more of the repetitive drudgery in large-scale systems, only the more professional tasks will be left for people to do. Professional people generally want more say in management, and possess more participatory skills, than the people who used to do the work machines can now do better. Hence all big organizations may come to be the way universities are—i.e., loose systems of self-governance in which most of the "employees" regard themselves as professional partners in general management.

People outside universities often have difficulty understanding university governance because they think of the organization as a pyramid in which the teachers "work for" the president or chancellor or whatever the chief executive is called. In practice, the faculty of a good university does not regard itself as responsible to the administrators in any hierarchical sense. Both faculty and administration are serving the university's purpose; the core of that purpose is academic; the natural leaders are therefore practicing intellectuals; and most of them are members of the faculty. The resulting arrangements for making decisions are better described in the language of legislative process than with words borrowed from business management or public administration.

The analogy between an academic faculty and a political legislature is apt. Every faculty member is juridically free and equal—a politically acceptable (if practically unrealistic) organization chart for a university faculty could be drawn only by placing all the names in a horizontal line on a long roll of paper. Both legislatures and faculties are, however, quite highly structured in terms of *de facto* power. Just as the influence of a Congressman is derived partly from the size of his vote in his home constituency, so a professor's position in the faculty is partly the product of his external repute in his own academic or professional field.

Despite the ample supply of administrators—in some institutions "overhead" takes up more than 50 percent of the salary budget—every faculty manages to retain for itself some real power to make important decisions, or at least to veto them. The minimum list might include tenure and promotion decisions, research leaves and other services to the faculty, revisions of the curriculum, approval of degrees including the honorary variety, legislation about the conditions of academic freedom, and initial jurisdiction in disciplinary cases. But in the structure of influence to handle such matters as these, a professor's national distinction as a scholar or his local repute as a lively teacher is by no means the major portion of his segmented ticket of admission to the elite. As in a legislature, seniority and long tenure are often important credentials for leadership. But personal effectiveness and skill in negotiation are usually the most important factors.

In faculty processes the familiar arts and crafts of legislation are much in evidence. Senatorial courtesy and logrolling, for example, have their analogies in the committee work on new courses, promotion-and-tenure decisions, and research grants. But academic faculties also are able to accomplish extraordinary feats of consensus, as legislatures do; issues which threaten to divide an academic community are often defused by open debate and settled by the constructive application of deliberate ambiguity.

Academic faculties share one other characteristic with legislatures—a pronounced willingness to delegate inherent powers to full-time administrators. The faculty's legislative processes are both cumbersome and resistant to change. As a consequence the change agents in large universities are increasingly those who handle money, manage resources, and are accountable in the eyes of outsiders for what happens on campus.

The tendency for important decisions to be left for the executives to handle is especially evident when there is a crisis. The rhetoric of "student power" and "faculty power" is much heard in periods of campus tranquillity. But in organization systems "power" is defined by the presence on one's desk of excruciating dilemmas requiring for their resolution the ability to communicate with all concerned and the willingness to take public responsibility for the outcome. At moments of crisis not very many student and faculty leaders are to be found beating down the university president's door in order to wrest those dilemmas from his grasp and take the heat involved in working them out. The buck flows toward the administrators. This is, of course, why university administration now matches city management as one of the nation's most precarious professions.

The leakage of "power" from academic faculties into the hands of executives parallels what is happening in state and national politics. The men who wrote the United States Constitution worried about giving the legislature too much power;

they warned of the "dangers from legislative usurpations," and created the separation of powers to prevent it. "One hundred and seventy-three despots would surely be as oppressive as one," James Madison said in one of *The Federalist* papers; ". . . an elective despotism was not the government we fought for." But complexity is sucking out of legislative bodies much of the real control of policy they used to have.

The Gulf of Tonkin Resolution, passed in the summer of 1964, was an outstanding example of a legislature's willingness to submit and enjoy the rape of its jurisdiction. President Johnson was running for re-election, which should have been suggestive at least to the Senate's Republican minority. The occasion for the Resolution was two minor naval engagements involving two American destroyers and some North Vietnamese torpedo boats in the Gulf of Tonkin. (The second engagement may have been even less significant than it seemed in the headlines of the day; later analysis revealed that some of the reported torpedoes may have been porpoises.) Yet U.S. Senators, with only two dissenting, were willing to give the President a blank check to use American combat forces in Southeast Asia. The later charge by some of the Senate's leaders that the President had deceived them does not explain how they were so readily hoodwinked into passing along to the President the Senate's constitutional right to participate in decisions about war and peace.

The Gulf of Tonkin Resolution is only a more dramatic incident in the growing imbalance in the constitutional separation of powers, not only in Washington but in the states as well. The new kinds of decisions to be made are so high in technological content, and so difficult for a part-time layman to analyze, that they tend to be left to "the experts"—and most of the experts are working for the executive branch of government. Government budgeting and fiscal management, traditionally the strongest stronghold of legislative power, is now so complex and computerized a specialty that only a few very experienced legislators can presume to argue with the professional budgeteers and economists. And in a growing number of states, the legislature has voluntarily divested itself of its traditional purse-string control by subjecting the bulk of the public budget to collective bargaining.

In Washington the Congress has become "the separate but unequal branch of the Federal Government," says Joseph A. Califano, Jr., once President Johnson's Special Assistant for Domestic Affairs. Congress is understaffed and badly organized for assessment of the technological complexities on which it is supposed to make policy. Up to 1971 Congress had acquired only four computers, and used them mostly for payrolls and administrative housekeeping; the executive branch had four thousand computers (all financed by Congress), working mostly on substantive policy. Califano spells it out: "The Pentagon, both within its own walls as well as in its think tanks like RAND and the Institute for Defense Analysis, can war-game any number of strategic or budgetary alternatives, while the Armed Services and Foreign Affairs Committees still base most of their decisions on the work of small staffs and the gut reactions and empirical idiosyncrasies of committee members. . . . The executive branch is by far the most significant force in the conception, development, and enactment into legislation of new substantive programs. The stark fact is that neither the Congress nor any of its committees has the consistent capability—without almost total reliance on the informational and analytical resources of the executive branch—of developing coherent, large-scale Federal programs." The same can be said, only more so, of most state legislatures and municipal councils.

The consequence is a pervasive blurring of the constitutional separation of powers. Just as major changes in a university's curriculum—a new professional school, a new kind of interdisciplinary program—often come from the administrators, so in government most of the laws are written not by the "lawmakers" but by the executives who will have to carry them out. In twenty years of off-and-on Federal service, I do not recall operating under any piece of legislation that was not written, in its essentials, in the executive branch. Meanwhile the members of Congress, relieved of some of the burdens of policy-making, spend a high proportion of their time influencing the way the laws are administered and who is appointed to administer them. (One of my first assignments, as a twenty-one-year-old intern in the office of Senator "Young Bob" La Follette, was to stand in for the Senator at a hearing in the Veterans Administration on a compensation case. The distortion of the separation of powers was plain to be seen: there I was, a legislative agent trying to influence the efforts of public executives to perform a judicial function.)

There is an obvious antidote: the Congress and other legislative bodies should hire large competent staffs and organize their own assessment of the technological and financial complexities. But it does not happen; individual legislators can easily see that the result might be a shift of jurisdiction from the executive bureaucracy to a legislative bureaucracy, but not necessarily an increase in the discretion of the individual legislator. At best, the establishment of staffs to compete with the executive would place more power in the hands of a few committee chairmen. And most legislators think their committee chairmen have too much power already—until they become committee chairmen themselves.

The fact that collective bodies such as political legislatures

43

and academic faculties are often willing to have Public Executives take the initiative in making technically complex and ethically difficult decisions should not be seen as an "upward" leakage of power. The leakage, like the relationship, is horizontal. Legislatures and faculties may be content to delegate outward the power to start things, but retain both the ambition and the ammunition to stop them. The political executive or university administrator who neglects to ask what they think, and listen hard to what they say, soon discovers that a decision which is later invalidated or changed because people who can enforce their right to be consulted were not consulted is not a decision at all.

All the formal power to govern a university is typically vested in a board of trustees or board of regents—a body of (usually unpaid) citizens who have to interpret the outside community to the academics and help protect the academic enterprise from the outsiders. Time was when these citizen boards were expected to raise the necessary dollars and otherwise display a passion for anonymity. But their overt participation in university governance is growing nowadays—and may provide a clue to the future role of boards of directors in business firms, philanthropic foundations, and professional partnerships.

Despite some of the rhetoric of higher education, a modern university is not a sanctuary; it is interconnected with its surrounding community in a thousand ways. The politics of university governance therefore go beyond the effort to achieve consensus within the university community. A public university depends on the taxpayers and the legislature and governor they elect; a private university is equally bound to maintain close relations with alumni and other outside givers; both kinds of universities engage in the Washington competitions which produce educational grants and research contracts.

The drive for "relevance" has intensified the intimacy between gown and town: students and faculty members sally forth to right the wrongs they perceive beyond the campus boundary, and find the wider community full of people with strong ideas about the wrongs they perceive on the campus. In an egalitarian society there is no such thing as a campus sanctuary from which it is all right for students and faculty to raid the outside world, but it is not all right for the outside world to help run the university. Members of every academic community are learning that they cannot have it both ways. If they presume to raise questions about international and national and local decisions, which as citizens they do and should, the international and national and local decision-makers will naturally raise questions about how professors work and students live. Those who want the protection of a monastery have to live like monks. On a relevant campus there's no hiding place down here.

The intermarriage of town and gown has placed new emphasis on the key role of the governing board. In organizations at the more "vertical" end of the spectrum of administration, it is still possible for the board of directors to be a cipher in the organization's decision-making. Often in private business and even in foundations, the board of directors is just another name for a committee dominated by members of the executive staff, plus some dependable former members of the management, plus a few—but not too many—representatives of large investors or major clients. But the wider the organization's public responsibility, and the broader the lateral consultations needed to fashion decisions that will "stick," the more necessary it is for the governing board to be drawn from a cross-section of people-in-general. Only such a board can bring to the internal policy deliberations a wider angle of vision, illuminating the issues of public responsibility which are the common preoccupation of "private" and "public" executives. And only such a board, when it goes out into the wider community to explain and justify (for example) the concept of academic freedom, will be a credible witness. If the university's board of trustees consisted mostly of students, professors, and deans, it obviously could not perform this function effectively.

The future executive will not be able to count on the passivity of citizen boards. Every large organization system will be deeply affected with the public interest; the next chapter will examine how far this is already true. It is a fair guess that before long a corporation or foundation which claims to be acting in the public's interest will be expected to demonstrate that its executives are accountable to a publicly responsible board that participates actively in establishing and revising the organization's subjective human purposes.

The university illustration suggests that the growing horizontalness of large organization systems, whatever their purpose, will require the future executive to accommodate to these facts of life:

· Clients, like students, will increasingly want to help make the key decisions that affect them.

· "Employees" will increasingly be professional people who think of themselves the way faculty members do, as part of management—and will behave more like legislators than like cogs in an executive hierarchy.

· Since all the constituencies except the central administration are organized as collective bodies, the hard political and ethical dilemmas will tend to be left to the executives.

They in turn will try through consultation to share their ethical burdens with clients, employees, trustees, and the public-at-large.

• As growing complexity requires an organization to take wider considerations and constituencies into account, it becomes necessary for the governing board to be drawn from the concerned outside publics, and not to be simply a redundant expression of the organization's internal dynamics.

The degree to which the world's work is accomplished horizontally will still vary, to be sure, according to what is administered. The spectrum of executive action will still range from organizations where at least some commands go down a hierarchical line to those in which nearly everything is done by horizontal negotiation among specialists and executives. A Marine platoon, together with family businesses and local trade unions, may still be found near one end of the continuum; hospitals, research labs, and academic faculties may remain the limiting cases of horizontal process. But Lesson No. 1 for the future executive is this: accelerating growth in the size and complexity of organization systems seems destined to move the whole spectrum away from the more formal, hierarchical, order-giving way of doing business and toward the more informal, fluid workways of bargaining, brokerage, advice and consent.

Chapter 4

The Blurring of "Public" and "Private"

The familiar blazes on the trees are being effaced, the marks made by those who trod the way before us are growing dim—the moral landmarks by which we traditionally have recognized such things as right and wrong.

—*Francis B. Sayre, Jr.*

As complexity feeds on growth and growth feeds on complexity, the decisions of large organizations affect more and more people, and those affected increasingly wonder why they should not therefore participate with the organization's managers in making those decisions. It is already true in the United States that the line between "public" and "private" can no longer be drawn between government and private enterprise, because all private enterprise has some degree of public responsibility—the larger and more complex the enterprise, the more public responsibility it is expected to carry. And this means that more and more private executives must simultaneously serve as Public Executives, whether they like it or not.

Stated thus baldly, this conclusion may seem obvious. Yet it is so far from being accepted doctrine that the public administrator and the private business executive normally treat themselves as separate categories. Their professional societies have almost nothing to do with each other. Their recruitment channels are quite separate. It is still quite difficult to transfer from one kind of career to the other. Their graduate training programs use quite different kinds of teaching materials, and no university anywhere in the industrialized world has successfully combined business and public administration into a single professional track in the interdisciplinary field of administration.

Yet the sheer size of the dominant structures in the "private" sector—corporations and banks and service agencies, the media and the foundations and private schools and colleges—will increasingly require those who join these structures to act as though they were responsible to the general public. Because they are.

Even compared to a generation ago, our private enterprise system is just as enterprising but not nearly so private. The growing sense of public responsibility in American business—verbalized at inspirational lunches but also increasingly in evidence during office hours—can be seen as the search for legitimacy by managers of properties whose "ownership" is no longer the key to executive responsibility.

It is now commonplace to observe that the diffusion of property divorces ownership from control of the economic system. Managers of productive enterprises, and managers of pension funds, mutual trusts, bank-held trusts and funds, and other large-scale forms of organized "private property," are each year harder put to it to say to whom they are effectively responsible. If the question is "Who owns General Motors or AT & T?" the honest answer is so vague an entity ("the public") that it leaves the collective leadership of managers in control of what is owned. To the more operational question, "Who is responsible for the actions of General Motors or AT & T?" the answer is clear enough: a large and growing number of their executives. But to whom are they responsible?

The issue about identity illustrated by these simple questions is paralleled in large-scale philanthropy and nonprofit enterprise. In a Ford Foundation or an American Cancer Society or a private university, as in most large corporations and financial institutions, some effort is usually made to separate powers between a legislative board of directors, or trustees, and a group of executive managers. But what the muckrakers of a generation ago used to call "interlocking directorates" are now more the rule than the exception—that is, the board of directors will be heavy with corporate vice presidents, major clients, alumni, contractors, benefactors, and others who can be expected to share the general orientation of the managerial group. Taking board members and top managers together, they often operate as a self-perpetuating oligarchy. As such they are responsible to each other and themselves—and therefore ultimately to people-in-general, which is to say to their own collective guess as to when public acquiescence will give way to public outrage.

People-in-general are not, however, very helpful in deciding questions of ethics and policy—how much profit to reinvest, when to build new plant, whether to merge with the competition, what prices are fair, how much to raise wages, what causes to promote through bank loans or foundation grants.

These decisions are made by sovereign individuals, their ethical responsibility obscured from outsiders (and sometimes from themselves) by complex committee work, what the Communists call "collective leadership."

What induces the Public Executives in private organizations to operate within acceptable boundaries (as measured by public outrage and consequent government intervention) is a double sanction—personal conscience, modified by external expectations about executive behavior. What tugs at the conscience, or outrages the relevant publics, is different in different places and even at different times in the same place. Twenty years ago most American businessmen felt no active responsibility for investing in black industry or training youngsters from the ghetto. Now many of them do, partly because they have come to feel some moral obligation to help solve a national problem that can no longer be ignored, and partly because they fear the social and corporate consequences if they fail to do their part. Ten years ago industries could dump waste in the rivers and oil in the oceans; but now a whole generation of converts to ecology are asking with Ralph Nader why, if individuals are forbidden by ordinance from relieving themselves in the nearest stream, this sensible antipollution rule should not apply to industries as well. I recently listened to a gas company executive describe all the antipollution equipment and procedures he was building into the specifications for a new refinery. "Ten years ago they would have thrown me out of the stockholders' meeting if I had suggested spending this kind of money to protect the public interest," he remarked. "Today they would throw me out if I *didn't* recommend all this public-interest spending."

For the responsible executive, the difference between working in a nominally private or an overtly public agency lies not so much in the kinds of ethical issues that arise as in the procedures available for judging whether they have been resolved to the public's taste. Executives in both environments have to unlock the same mysteries, imply in their decisions the same kinds of answers to ultimate questions: how to reconcile efficiency with humanity, how to promote full employment without undue inflation, how much is "sufficiency," what prices to charge and pay, what costs to incur now for what benefits later on, how hard to press toward undefinable goals, how fast to grow, which direction is up.

In a public agency questions like these which touch the organization's ultimate purposes are no less pressing, no less inherent in day-to-day decisions, no less difficult to answer than are the analogous enigmas in a private business. But they do not create the same sense of moral crisis because there is a legitimate, agreed-upon *procedure* for answering them. The opinion of people-in-general is ultimately consulted (sometimes much too late, to be sure) by counting votes in a general election or in a legislature which for the manager's purpose is defined as "representative" no matter how unrepresentative it may in practice be. But in private enterprise, profit and nonprofit, the public interest is not authoritatively determined. The public interest is what the managers think it is—unless they so outrage their relevant publics that they bring government regulation on themselves.

People-in-general exercise their ultimate power most decisively by making private managers responsible to the government, in a single act which both justifies and monitors the managers' power over large organizations affected with the public interest. Such decisions stretch in a long line from the nationalization of the Post Office and the public utility holding company acts, through the Federal Communications Act and the efforts to bring labor unions under governmental regulation, down to the fights to enforce fair-employment practices and destroy racial discrimination in education and housing. Government participation in higher education, through subsidies for research and training, has made private universities think hard about their dependence on what voters and elected officials may do to their autonomy if aroused.

Even private philanthropy, which long had the greatest autonomy, has now fallen afoul of adverse reaction by people-in-general, acting mostly through the power to tax and to exempt from taxes. It started seriously in 1961, when Congressman B. Carroll Reece conducted an unfriendly investigation of some of the big foundations, arguing that tax "exemptions are acts of grace by the Federal Government . . . the Federal Government permits the equivalent of public moneys to be used by these foundations. Accordingly, it is justified in applying . . . such conditions on the exemptions as may be calculated to prevent abuse of the privilege and to prevent the use of the exempted funds against the public interest."

The foundations were eloquent in describing the good things they were doing, but they never really found a persuasive counterdoctrine. The best they could do was to invoke a vague constitutional protection and then argue that their own "high duty of public responsibility" was as effective a safeguard against abuse as any conceivable form of government regulation.

The 1960s saw a spectacular growth in the number and resources of private foundations, including many which were patently tax dodges and a few which were obviously meddling in elective politics. The Ford Foundation's rather casual decision to give research grants to several Kennedy Administration alumni touched off an effort to include in a tax reform

53

bill provisions to control the amounts spent by tax-exempt foundations and proscribe some categories of spending. The issue became so complicated that the central moral and political issue—if foundations are responsible to the public, how does the public monitor the exercise of that responsibility?— ran out into the sands of legal technicality. But the issue remains, sharpening the foundations' self-questions about each action they take in the public's name.

To avoid the embarrassment of undue restrictions on their freedom of action, the Public Executives in American corporate enterprise and private nonprofit organizations are reacting in ways that further blur the distinction between "public" and "private."

First, the managers intensify the practice of "collective leadership." As we have seen, this is necessary for technological reasons anyway; growing bigness, growing complexity of relations, and more specialization of function multiply the interrelated decisions to be made and diffuse the power to make them. Major decisions are typically made by an executive committee, often in tandem with a finance committee or other groups of executives. This obscures the personal accountability for major decisions which, because they are of interest to the public, are likely to be controversial. It is, for example, rare to find a price increase announced personally by a top official of a modern corporation.

Second, the managers maintain a curtain of public relations, with an increasing emphasis on "institutional advertising" to build an image of a good-guy corporation taking the public's quite legitimate interests fully into account. Those who do not show forth their interest in conservation, ecology, safety, economy, planning, beauty, and culture risk regulation to enforce it.

The Blurring of "Public" and "Private"

In a third response to the "public" imperative, the executives in private organizations are arranging to bring the government into their affairs as a risk-taking partner. This trend is so familiar that it scarcely needs to be spelled out here. Atomic energy, aerospace, communications, housing and urban redevelopment, health delivery, soil conservation, the savings bank business, foreign investment guarantees, research and development in nearly every field—the list could be indefinitely extended. For the private side of the bargain, it is a profitable but perilous partnership; government aims and policies can shift suddenly. The fate of a regional industry may hang on a few votes in one house of Congress, as the debates over antiballistic missile systems and supersonic aircraft illustrated in 1970 and 1971. A change in direction—cutbacks in the space program and the decline of military procurement for Vietnam are recent examples—can blight whole industries; the largest companies are developing quotas of government business to protect them from fluctuations in public policy. In higher education a major financial crisis occurs whenever the Department of Defense cuts back on R & D funds, the National Science Foundation changes its priorities, or the National Institutes of Health have their appropriation reduced.

Because public policy is thus an element in business planning, the managers of American corporations find it logical to intervene more frequently and more deeply in the processes by which governments make up their multiple minds. If business executives are responsible not only for running their own businesses but for preventing depressions, competing with the European Common Market, and defending the U.S. against the Soviet Union, then they must participate in setting interest rates, controlling government spending, allocating government subsidies to the right interests, planning defense production, and managing U.S. foreign policy. If business firms are going to be held responsible for progress in their own urban communities, their managers had better interest themselves in the honesty of local government and the rehabilitation of "downtown." If the state legislatures are going to regulate the insurance business, the managers of insurance companies had better try even harder to regulate the state legislatures.

The process is ill described by the old-fashioned word "lobbying," which to most people means influencing legislators. Since most important legislation is now written in the executive departments of government, the power of new-style lobbies can be most accurately measured by the strength of their "representatives" within the *executive* bureaucracy.

The blurring of "public" and "private" makes it hard to draft a law or write a rule against conflict of interest that applies to any but the minor cases of corruption in office. The big interests of industry and government are not even seen to be in conflict. (It was not Charles Wilson's first statement— "What's good for the country is good for General Motors"— that got him into trouble, but the fact that he added, ". . . and vice versa.") It is considered normal and natural for a steel man to lubricate with government contracts the growth of steel production; for a housing man to get more housing built by having the government absorb as much of the risk as possible; for a farmers' representative to promote aid for farmers from inside the Department of Agriculture; for a labor organizer temporarily in the government to promote the right of labor to organize. We have institutionalized the inside track.

Aggression across the disappearing frontier between "public" and "private" does not all come from the private side. If business finds advantage in getting the government to take on business risks, government finds it equally advantageous to share with the business community the risk of political flak and administrative error.

The Public Executives in government at every level have two contradictory aims. On the one hand, we the people expect public agencies to take on many new or expanded functions, to do what is not being done enough or well enough in the "private sector," and to do some things (such as build a Strategic Air Command) for which responsibility cannot by its nature be delegated to private individuals or organizations. The trouble is that growing social complexity, the product of scientific invention and technological innovation, has greatly increased the proportion of the world's work which "the people cannot as well do for themselves." The growth of large aggregations of "private" power, notably the corporations, has partly filled this gap. But even the exercise of corporate power is often in practice the result of governmental initiative.

On the other hand, we the people all agree that government should not become a bloated bureaucracy. We laugh at the tendency of government to grow, and call it Parkinson's Law; but we worry about it, too.

Thus government, trying not to grow but also trying to meet the people's expectations, farms out to private organizations (business firms, research organizations, and nonprofit agencies) a very large part of the "public business." Most of the nation's taxes are now collected not by government but by private organizations, through the withholding device. Most of our military production is not undertaken, as it used to be, through government "arsenals," but through private corporations which do most or in some cases all of their business with the United States Department of Defense. The management of the Post Office has been reorganized in corporate form. A growing proportion of the foreign-aid program is farmed out to nongovernment contractors. The heavy use of the government's contracting power in such programs as atomic energy and space exploration suggests that major technological departures from now on, in our continuing Scientific Revolution, will continue to be the product of government initiative with little private risk-taking.

Even if private enterprise had less incentive to drag government into risk-taking partnership, legislators and Public Executives on the government side would find advantages in propping up private corporations with subsidies and guarantees, to spread the risk of political criticism that would attend a production function undertaken directly by the government. When these arrangements become very large, it is very hard to tell where the private interest intersects with the public: the Lockheed Corporation in the United States and Rolls-Royce in Britain both found in 1971 that cost overruns on a jetliner placed their very existence at the mercy of politics in Washington and London.

The advantage of farming out the public business is so great that governments have spawned private corporations to do public business in a private tent under government contract. A notable case was of course the RAND Corporation, established by the Department of the Air Force for research and development purposes; it became an effective public thinking machine, in private corporate form, and even developed some clients outside the military establishment. Similarly, when the Department of Defense decided to set up a training program for the officers destined to staff its Military Assistance Advisory Groups abroad, it created a private corporation, staffed with retired military officers, as a more flexible administrative device able to pay higher salaries than any government agency.

Illustrations of the trend are not all to be found in the Department of Defense. In the housing field, subsidies and guarantees to private builders and housing financers have generally been better politics than "public housing," which is both financed and managed by government officials. When the government is able to delegate a public responsibility through the contracting device, that also helps the Public Executives in government share with the Public Executives in "private" organizations the discredit for the administrative troubles, delays, and complaints which attend any large-scale undertaking.

How successful the farming out of public functions can be was illustrated with televised drama when Apollo IX reached the Moon within the deadline set by President Kennedy eight years before. The feat of the three astronauts was the product of some 300,000 persons, most of them working in "private" organizations, effectively coordinated to serve a clear public purpose. But most publicly financed systems do not have as visible an objective as the Moon.

The existence side by side of "private" and "government" organizations performing generally the same functions tends to produce pressures for the government to prop up the private organizations so they can survive in the face of the government's unlimited resources. In a situation where the government has to ensure continuing economic growth, yet keep economic power diffused in many hands, the arguments about public policy and the political infighting that accompanies them have to do with just where the line will be drawn between direct government operation and indirect forms of public participation in private enterprise.

For example, Congress and some of the state legislatures

are annually grappling with the issue of government aid for private, particularly parochial, schools. If people-in-general are going to take responsibility, through their government, for transporting children to public schools and feeding them hot lunches when they get there, should not the government help transport children to private schools and feed them lunch, too? Governments are gradually assuming this kind of responsibility, using the rationale that public schools should not put private schools out of business. Similar discussions are going on in the field of higher education, in connection with government aid to private colleges and universities. The trend is toward finding ways for the government to pump budget money into private universities without appearing to interfere with the universities' control over academic standards, faculty self-government, or even student discipline. World-wide, the most successful prototype of a public "buffer" between government and higher education is the University Grants Commission in Britain.

Government also encourages private organizations to engage in activities which are good public policy but could not be defended as government functions. While I was managing Far Eastern foreign aid for the Economic Cooperation Administration, the Burmese Government requested American help to enable the University of Rangoon to celebrate the 2,500th anniversary of the Buddha. My colleagues and I tried to imagine ourselves explaining to Congressmen from the Bible Belt why the taxpayers' money was being used to celebrate the Buddha's birthday. At about that time Paul Hoffman, who had been administering the foreign-aid program, was appointed president of the Ford Foundation. We suggested he take the project with him, and the U.S. eventually derived some political credit in Burma from a large Peace Pagoda financed with automobile profits—without a row in Washington.

There are those who, observing that much of the marginal risk in our business system is now assumed by people-in-general through their government, conclude that America is finding its way to socialism through the back door. This is, for example, the conclusion of Yugoslavia's economic planners, in a study of the U.S. economy. They argue that it is now unnecessary to have a cold war with the capitalists, since the capitalists are moving so rapidly toward socialism under their own steam. (The Yugoslavs are not equally impressed with the rapid movement toward the introduction of capitalist-type incentives in their own government-dominated economy.)

It is true that our mixed-up public/private business system is not well described by the mid-nineteenth-century word "capitalism," or even by the twentieth-century concepts of monopolistic competition. But it is also nonsense to try to fit the American economy into the mid-nineteenth-century word "socialism," let alone its twentieth-century totalitarian variant. The socialist countries have been learning in their own ways that it does not matter very much who theoretically "owns" the means of production; the question is who controls them. They do not yet believe in a system where nobody is in charge —though they, too, are being pushed by technology into a wider dispersal of initiative and control.

Most Americans do take as an article of faith that more dispersal of public power protects the public weal, and that leads to placing public functions in private managerial hands. There is nothing wrong with this *if* the "private" Public Executives who handle them act as if they are accountable to the public for both their efficiency and their ethics. We will consider in Chapter 8 how the blurring of old distinctions requires us to invent new ways to keep faith with what Adolph Berle called those "odd American notions that absolute power should not exist, that countervailing power ought to be maintained and that legitimacy of any power must rest upon a popular base."

Part Two

Qualities

Chapter 5

Ladders to Leadership

In the midst of all stands the leader, gathering, as best he can, the thoughts that are completed—that are perceived—that have told upon the common mind; judging also of the work that is now at length ready to be completed . . . perceiving the fruits of toil and of war—and combining all these into words of progress, into acts of recognition and completion. . . . Who shall say that this is not an exalted function? Who shall dispraise the title of leadership?

—*Woodrow Wilson*

The future is shocking and man's survival in jeopardy: that is the message of the best of nonfiction in the early 1970s. Disaster so predictable suggests a savior—to build an ark, to lead us out of the wilderness, to revise our aspirations and revive our faith. But it is in the nature of complexity that no one savior will do. The requirement is for multiple Messiahs. In a society based on large-scale organization systems, needing even larger-scale systems to domesticate new technologies, the operational Messiahs will mostly be the Public Executives, the men and women whose function is to bring people together to make something happen in the public interest.

We have guessed at the environment these future executives will share: complex public/private bundles of relations, held together by constructive tensions, styled for horizontal consensus rather than vertical command. The rest of this book will focus on the Public Executive as an individual. What are his or her ladders to leadership? What attitudes and aptitudes will future executives share in common? How can they maintain a sense of exhilaration? Who, or what, holds the Public Executive's feet to the fire of public responsibility? How does the Public Executive leader work out his or her own personal sense of direction? What firmly believed premises had the Public Executive better question, and revise? And, in a world of bigness and complexity, how can the Public Executive be free?

We are accustomed to thinking of leaders as few among many. But the history of hierarchical governance is a poor guide to the age of consultation and consensus that has already begun.

In the ancient world Pericles and a handful of other Greeks set styles in politics and architecture which remain with us today in political lore and utterance, and in the grace of many a public building. Lorenzo the Magnificent did not need a very large group of cronies to set the style of the Renaissance in Florence; when his son Piero was overthrown and a republic formed, leadership passed to advisory intellectuals like Machiavelli—but they, too, were few in number.

Modern civilization has long since abandoned the principle

that a community should be governed and styles should be set by the merely rich and highly born. Yet there persists today, in most of the world, a pyramidal social structure in which a relatively few men and women—mostly men, which is one of the problems—are in general charge. The revolutions of the eighteenth and nineteenth centuries, and the anticolonial movement of the twentieth, typically cast out small groups of bosses in favor of other small groups of bosses, ruling with no greater consent of the governed. Those who talked most about devolving power to the people seemed most anxious to concentrate power in the hands of the few.

But somewhere along the way in the modernized, industrialized, "developed" nations and especially in the United States of America, rule by the few became technologically obsolete. The more interrelated are the parts of an economy, a polity, and a culture, the more people it takes to run things. Each year it takes a greater *proportion* of leaders to participate in socially significant decisions—because each year there are so many new kinds of decisions to be made, and so many more concerned groups that feel they have a right to be cut in on the decision-making. Even in the totalitarian societies the notion of effective "dictatorship" is breaking down. The dynamics of development loosen the up-and-down controls, and spread the responsibility for initiative and follow-through to hundreds, then thousands, then tens of thousands of "cadres."

In the mid-1950s I tried to count America's "opinion leaders," because I was publisher of a magazine I thought they ought to read. (Other publications later adopted parallel appeals to "the influentials," "the men who get ahead," and the like.) My 1955 estimate was 555,000; a similar analysis of "opinion leaders" might yield as many as one million in 1971. The concept of "opinion leaders" is broader than that of Public

Executives, since the former also includes teachers, artists, doctors, lawyers, judges, legislators, and other professional people as well. But the Public Executives—policy-makers in public, philanthropic, voluntary, and large-scale "private" enterprise—were about seven out of ten of the "opinion leaders" in the earlier estimate. They might thus be 700,000 out of 200,000,000 Americans in 1971. Before long the Public Executives will number a million in the United States alone.

What no Greek political theorist imagined or people's revolutionary accomplished—a devolution of real power to hundreds of thousands of people—is coming to pass as the social consequence of modern science and technology. We have our aristocracy, but it is increasingly an aristocracy of achievement. By common consent we no longer entrust the setting of styles to any one class, any one race, any one priesthood or courthouse gang—or even to the White House staff. The destiny decisions we face are so terribly important they cannot be left to the experts, the wealthy, the products of the Ivy League, or the residents of the Eastern Seaboard. For a generation it has been conventionally wise to predict that more complex technologies would make for more centralization of leadership. My impression is the opposite: complexity of organization systems is diffusing the opportunity to lead and multiplying the requirement for leaders.

There is no career ladder called "leadership." The contributors to our socially significant decisions most often achieve their sway by first climbing the ladder of their chosen specialty. They become leading lawyers, leading businessmen, leading labor organizers, leading clergymen, leading rebels, leading educators, leading racketeers, leading publicists, leading artists, leading civil servants or politicians—or they achieve prominence as civic leaders by doing unpaid chores or asking awkward questions in their own communities. Even in public administration, for which a generalist outlook is claimed, the typical career starts with five or ten years of specialized work on the management side of government.

"We have a preference," said Arthur Koestler in *The Anatomy of Snobbery*, ". . . for people who are likely to leave their imprint on our time. Whether they leave their imprint as politicians, Chinese scholars, or collectors of snuffboxes does not matter. . . . To be oneself is not enough; one must be 'somebody.' "

The somebodies of the future will bear little resemblance to the contemporary caricature of The Establishment—a few elderly moneyed manipulators calling the tune for the rest of us. The coming Establishment will contain all kinds of people, many not tapped by others but self-selected—including the anti-Establishment leaders who are organizing to take over some of the old Establishment's power. Black Panthers and members of the Council on Foreign Relations will both be eligible. The future Establishment will be not only very large but very fluid, its composition changing daily as new arrivals breaking out of their specialties into general leadership overtake those who die, retire, or drop out of the aristocracy of achievement because they weary of its demands. There are still too many ethnic, economic, and regional exceptions, but the future-oriented rule is that anybody can be a somebody, if he or she has the talent and is willing to work at it.

Most of us resist the notion that it is important to be "somebody." The ideal, surely, is to be oneself. This complaint against the overrated dignities of high society, the pomposities of politics, and the inequalities of opportunity is thoroughly justified. But it is often, nowadays, carried to the point of rejecting any personal role in fixing what is wrong and curing what is sick about modern society. There is room on the beaches, in the parks, and in the wilderness for a large number of people who think that dropping out of society is the way to be oneself. But there is another, more relevant way to be oneself—to throw oneself into the effort to accomplish what one deeply believes needs to be accomplished.

If some of the children of the affluent upper middle classes race toward the wilderness rather than toward the centers of decision, there are plenty of other young people, not so affluent and not so bored with having it made, who will fill our growing national requirement for aristocrats of achievement. It will not be the first time in history that the children of a too-satisfied Establishment have been elbowed aside by the children of the upward mobile.

Somewhere on the climb from oneself to somebody, the leader passes an invisible line and something happens—not so much to him as to the expectations of those who surround him. He begins to be regarded as a kind of oracle on many topics beyond the range of his experience, beyond his competence to form a considered opinion on his own. The reason for this is straightforward enough. Most people are apathetic about most subjects—they have to be, there are so many subjects. François Rabelais, more than four hundred years ago, may have been the last man to believe that he could learn everything important there was to know—and have a good time besides. We all leave to "authorities" a growing share of our thinking about science and technology, about literature and the arts, and about economics and public affairs.

These "authorities" are mostly not experts on public affairs, but somebodies who have risen to prominence as specialists in something else, and remained to pontificate on a wide spectrum of topics to which they cannot have given professional attention. A construction engineer in Boston contracts to go to the Middle East for a few months to supervise the building of a bridge. Soon after his return the engineer goes to a cocktail party and is promptly surrounded by an eager cluster of friends. "What about the situation in the Middle East?" they want to know. He resists the pressure at first: "Don't ask *me*. I was just building a bridge." But within a month, after a few more such gatherings, we find him the center of an interested circle, explaining how to make peace between Israel and the Arabs. His skill as a builder and his willingness to travel have converted him into an opinion leader on war and peace.

The trouble with promoting people through specialized achievement to positions of leadership in matters of public policy is that the resulting leaders do not necessarily stop thinking as experts. It is hard enough for a specialist to predict the rate and direction of change even in his field, not only because the future is inherently uncertain but because he cannot possibly know enough about all the trends in other fields of expertness which may deeply affect the trend-lines he really understands.

If you know something about a subject, you instinctively take with a grain of salt what the experts on that subject tell you. We have all had enough experience with practical meteorology—that is, we have all picnicked in the rain on days predicted to be sunny—so that we approach the weatherman's forecast with an appropriate degree of skepticism. The same kind of skepticism would be justified in judging all expert forecasts, but if the field of analysis is unfamiliar to us, we are tempted to take more seriously what the experts say. The next flawed step is to depend on the specialized somebodies to sort out for us the general policy implications of what is happening with such bewildering rapidity in their own and a hundred other branches of science and society. Nuclear physicists speak up on disarmament, doctors lecture us on health insurance, statisticians prescribe birth control, industrialists give opinions on government budgeting. There is no inherent reason why specialists should be notably good at analyzing the implications for general policy of what is happening even in the fields they know, and many of them are not.

That is why a successful specialist, passing the dotted line which marks him off as a leader, often finds himself in deep moral and intellectual trouble. The qualities which have caused him to stand out from a crowd of experts are likely not to be the same as those required to meet the expectations of a wider constituency for general leadership. In the rarefied environment of public policy, the continuous subdivision of knowledge is matched by the need for a more and more intimate interrelationship of every specialty with every other specialty. If he is going to exercise his influence, the "influential" needs to develop a kind of competence that was typically not featured in the education that qualified him for the climb up his chosen ladder. The new skill is in bringing experts together in organization systems, to make judgments and take actions that none of them could manage alone.

The paradox of our not-so-manifest destiny is here. The control panels where expertness is married to purpose must be manned by an aristocracy of specialized achievement. Yet our scarcest resource appears to be men and women who have the incentive to grow beyond their specialized fields, who have some understanding of the administrative process, who are challenged rather than repelled by complexity.

72

Ladders to Leadership

On the one hand science has made possible continuous change at an accelerating rate, accompanied by growing interdependence of social decisions, growing hugeness of organization systems, and growing diffusion of power within and among them. The major obstacle to the next stage in America's success story is obviously our inability to "get it all together." Getting it all together requires a rapidly expanding ration of executive leaders, and an even larger number of people able to understand the policy issues, relate them to each other, and serve as opinion leaders outside their own fields of expertise.

Yet it has been the practice of modern civilization to place such stress on the division of labor as to siphon off into relatively narrow specialties nearly all of the first-rate talent. A young man or woman building a career can envision the excitement of the laboratory or the construction job, the hospital or the department store, the scholar's study or the teacher's classroom. Close attention to the situation as a whole is set aside by most college students by the end of their sophomore year, if indeed they did not start concentrating on nursing or electronics or auto mechanics or accounting before that. Even if a young man or woman aspires to a "generalist" role as politician or public executive, he or she can readily perceive that the ladders to leadership are the specialties and professions. Ten years later one can hardly blame them if they have come to prefer the shelter of expertise to the risky role of leadership. It is easier to be an expert, with the obligation merely to be right, than to be a leader, with the obligation to fuse a dozen forms of rigid rectitude into relevant action.

In 1957, when the Russians' first Sputnik set off an agonized reappraisal of American education, a rare and sensible voice was raised by a committee of citizens under the chairmanship of John Gardner. It suggested a substitute for the tearing of hair and rending of garments which had become, and remain today, so prevalent among seers and prophets in education. The Gardner Report did not complain about specific shortages in mathematicians, scientists, technologists, and people who speak exotic languages—which shortages had just been declared by Act of Congress to be the main trouble with American higher education. The Gardner Report did not worry at all about our capacity to produce first-rate experts at will. Instead, it saw in the short supply of "gifted generalists" the prime bottleneck in U.S. manpower and womanpower planning:

> The trend toward specialization has created among other things an extraordinary demand for gifted generalists—men with enough intellectual technical competence to deal with the specialists and enough breadth to play more versatile roles, whether as managers, teachers, interpreters or critics. Such individuals will be drawn increasingly from the ranks of those whose education and experience have included *both* depth and breadth—who have specialized but have not allowed themselves to become imprisoned in their specialty.
>
> . . . there is a premium on men and women with a talent for innovations, for individuals who can move beyond the limits of present practice. In a time of breathtaking technological and social changes there is a need for people who understand the process and the nature of change and who are able to cope with it. . . . We should educate our young people to meet an unknown need rather than to prepare them for needs already identified.

The wisdom of this passage survives fifteen years of dust on the report itself. If each year there are more and more decisions to be made, if the organization systems needed to make them are more and more complex, it follows that the rate at which general executives are produced had better be greater than any other growth rate in our society.

Chapter 6

A Style for Complexity

The greater you are, the humbler you must be.
—*Ecclesiasticus 3:18*

When a university starts looking for a new president, a government leader needs a new political executive, or a large private organization seeks an executive for a major assignment, a group of trustees or advisers or management consultants is often asked to write down the specifications for the person sought. They find this deceptively easy to do; the trouble is, their list of desired qualities is likely to describe the Angel Gabriel. Having satisfied themselves that the paragon they really want is otherwise employed, members of the search committee belatedly begin to look for a fallible, flesh-and-blood human being.

If I now derive from my projection of the executive environ-

75

ment a profile of the future executive, I risk tumbling into a similar trap. A million Americans cannot be said to be all alike even in one respect, let alone in many. Yet if you look around at the American Public Executives you know, and focus on those you would regard as especially effective, you will find a striking similarity in certain qualities and points of style.

The most obvious of these is physical energy. Executive tasks typically involve long hours and much homework. The broader the responsibility, the harder it is to "leave it at the office." The executive is seldom able to say that something he is doing is finished and is therefore not to be worried about any more. Dr. Mottram Torre, who has brooded for years about the dangers of psychiatric disability in high office, lists three common characteristics of "high energy level personalities": a significant skill in channeling energy, the ability to conserve energy by projecting the blame to others in the making of decisions, and the ability to release energy and relax.

Almost any physical or mental illness diminishes vitality and heightens self-concern. For an executive, serious illness results in a lowered interest in his work, a tendency to shut out new information (he feels he has too much already), further analysis (the problems on his plate are already more complicated than the human spirit can bear), and uncomfortable peers (who likely will ask him to think some more rather than decide on the basis of what he already thinks). In an environment of accelerating change and compounding complexity, such insulation from the new, the complicated, and the uncomfortable may cause the ill executive to pursue unsuccessful lines of action, which he might have changed were he healthy, alert, and fully informed. Any large organization is witness to dozens of examples in the course of a year. Our political history shows how crucial it can be for a public official to be feeling well at moments of destiny—Franklin Roosevelt's performance at Yalta ("He won't take any interest in what we are trying to do," Churchill complained), Woodrow Wilson's tactical rigidity when he was bedridden yet still President, Lincoln's damaging hesitations during the first year of his Presidency ("When hurried by the pressure of rapidly changing, uncontrollable circumstances and events, he tended to become . . . inwardly indecisive," says historian Edward J. Kempf).

Beyond the animal energy required to be a change agent in an environment of extreme complexity, the Public Executives of the future will, I think, be marked by a set of attitudes and aptitudes which seem to be necessary for the leadership of equals, which is the key to the administration of complexity. They will be more intellectual, more reflective, than the executives of the past; they will be "low-key" people, with soft voices and high boiling points; they will show a talent for consensus and a tolerance for ambiguity; they will have a penchant for unwarranted optimism; and they will find private joy in public responsibility.

It used to be said that a good executive could always hire brains; other executive qualities were harder to come by. Thirty years ago Barnard listed intelligence last, and it seemed reluctantly, among the talents required. There may still be training programs which teach that the executive's main task is to get good men and delegate them full responsibility for clearly defined pieces of the work to be done. But modern complexity has rendered this conventional wisdom both unconventional and unwise. The system executive is acutely aware that none of the pieces of the work can be clearly defined, and most of them are not even clearly within his jurisdiction. The effective executive no longer asks for "completed staff work" on important matters; he must immerse his own mind in the staff work, because he knows that it is in the staff work that policy decisions are made.

The executive's work often consists in meeting a series of unforeseeable obstacles on the road to an objective which can be clearly specified only when he is close to reaching it. He tries to imagine the unforeseen by posing contingencies and asking how his organization system would adjust if they arose. But the planned-for contingency never happens; something else happens instead. The planning therefore does not produce a usable plan, but something more precious: people better trained to analyze the unpredicted and to winnow out for the decision-makers (plural, as already noted) the choices that would be too costly to fudge or postpone.

This requires that the participating experts and staff assistants acquire some understanding of what it is like to be a Public Executive, how it feels to frame a decision that will "stick." But it also demands that the decision-makers themselves participate in the staff work, try to understand the expert testimony, measure the options and filter the imagined consequences of each through their best computers, which are their own minds. Even in "collective research" the breakthrough ideas usually turn out to be the product of one man's brooding, of his reading, of the sudden inspiration that fits together in a usable pattern the random data and partial reasoning of others—an idea honed in the darkest hours of the night by that marvelous instrument, the individual human mind.

Anyone who has worked with organized systems has to be impressed with the capacity of the human brain to cope with complexity. Viewed as a sensitive computer not limited to quantified "bits," the brain is able to take in a wide range of observations, weigh them according to their multiple relevance, store them in a memory of fantastic dimensions, retrieve them with high speed and reasonable accuracy, organize them into options, come up with a line of action, and transmit instructions to other parts of the body in a fraction of a second. Even so, an organization system by definition is too ramified for any one executive's mind to encompass. But the executive can comprehend the relations among its parts and its people, and can concentrate that energy of his on the parts that are not working well, or which are not yet routinized.

The future executive will therefore be something of an intellectual, not only by training but by temperament as well. If the executive is not himself plowing through the analysis, he is not making decisions; he is merely presiding while others decide. The obligation to think hard, fast, and free is the one executive function that cannot be delegated.

As the future executive tests his brain against his corner of complexity, he will find that certain techniques of leadership work best. The hallmarks of this modern style are the soft voice and the low key.

The signs are already much in evidence. The manners of a dean toward his faculty in a good university are spreading in domains where standing at attention is still in living memory. Even near the more "vertical" end of the spectrum of administration, in infantry divisions, fighter squadrons, and warships at sea, the men who are running things find less and less need for a loud voice or a parade-ground manner. If they want to reach large numbers of people, they order up an electronic amplifier. If they have orders to give to subordinates, they are more and more likely to call a meeting and act by consensus— or at least to formulate the command as a suggestion. In Israel this point is illustrated with the story of an Israeli battalion performing a drill in honor of a visiting dignitary. In a quiet voice the commander gave the order: "Battalion march." The visitor was surprised. "You have to shout the order," he said, "so they all start together." The commander smiled tolerantly. "The word will get around," he replied.

While working in Europe I had occasion to visit a number of military posts related to the NATO defense system. It was hard to avoid the conclusion that a growing proportion of each officer's time is spent dealing horizontally with people who are not "under" or "over" him. The infantry captain who calls in air support of his beleaguered company is not dealing up and down a chain of command, but negotiating across several chains of command. The colonel designated as "base commander" may find representatives of fifteen or twenty different U.S. military organizations camping on the two square miles of "his" base. None of these units is responsible to him; they deal with him laterally, as a tenant deals with a landlord. In the military as elsewhere, the more complicated things become, the more each "decision-maker" is consulting, bargaining, clearing with people he cannot order around and who cannot order him around. The changes in executive style which horizontalness makes mandatory brings military administration each day closer to the administration of hospitals, higher education, and scientific research.

The more critical the function and the more split-second the timing, the more likely you are to find in charge individuals with a relaxed appearance who direct by indirection and confer the maximum personal responsibility on each staff member. If you sit above the flight deck of an aircraft carrier, watching the "air boss" at work, you find him depending heavily on the extemporaneous originality, the ability to adapt known procedures to unknown emergencies, of every member of his staff. He is responsible for planes being catapulted from the deck and safely landed on it, an intricate and dangerous function. Yet the air boss infrequently gives an order; most of the time he is monitoring a complex but familiar procedure, intervening only when he sees trouble developing which the men running around on the deck cannot see. Since the flight deck in use is noisy, the key participants in its choreography are wired for sound. The air boss can hear what they say to each other, and that is how most of the work gets done; he can pre-empt a decision, wave off an incoming plane, or call up reinforcements to handle a crisis. But the system would not work at all if it depended on cumbersome vertical recommendations and approvals. Each man is using his own judgment, sharpened by training to be sure, while the air boss watches, monitors, calculates, thinks ahead—and feels no need to prove his virility by shouting, even in the presence of visitors.

The new style is also a technological necessity. Down in the bowels of the aircraft carrier, there is a large, dimly lit room full of serious young men bent over radar screens which show the position of all aircraft and surface vessels in the general vicinity; around the wall are displayed masses of current data, from the name and location of the nearest alternate landing field to the latest calculation of how much jet fuel each plane aloft has remaining in its tanks. Information about the drama above decks is exchanged in quiet, unemotional tones. The lesson for executive style is plain: Complexity of operation magnifies small errors and makes the whole system vulnerable. People who get too easily excited are likely to get in the way, and will be asked to simmer down regardless of rank.

The degree to which this new style has taken hold in the armed services must vary greatly according to the function to be performed. A complicated planning assignment is likely to be handled in a more collegial mode than the taking of a hill by a company of infantry. But even in the most vertical structures officers can no longer be quite as certain as they might have been a generation ago that an order automatically produces the consent to follow it. Some traces of participatory democracy are to be found in some of the most effective platoons.

It is functional for a Public Executive to be "low-key" because his unique function is to develop consensus around a subjective human purpose. As larger systems are organized to assess and control for man the innovations of technology, the new systems will require of their managers an even more collegial, consensual style. And as this trend gains momentum, it will render obsolescent in executive process the decision-making procedure we in the Western world have considered the heart of democracy—choosing up two sides and voting.

Two-sidedness is built deep into Western culture. We would experience a kind of culture shock if we saw more than two boxers in a ring, more than two teams on an athletic field, more than two sides in a collective bargaining session, more than two adversaries litigating in a courtroom, more than two parties in a legislature. Yet in problem-solving outside these artificial constructs there is almost no such thing as a two-sided problem. A two-sided analysis of the Arab-Israeli conflict, a corporate price rise, or an issue in university governance is a nonsense analysis.

For a week while I was in the State Department, I conducted an empirical test of two-sidedness: for every foreign-policy issue that reached my desk, I asked myself how many different sides were interested and engaged. My conclusion hardly rates as a scientific finding, though it carries the prestige of quantification: on the average, each of the issues I dealt with in Washington that week had 5.3 sides.

In a complex organization system, even the pretense of two-sidedness would be ridiculous. The Public Executive pursues his subjective human purpose by persuasion and consensus; he knows by instinct that an orderly two-sided debate on any important issue is bound to confuse consideration of a five-sided problem and inhibit the process of bringing people together in large systems to make things happen. Robert's *Rules of Order* is at best useless in building the kinds of organizations required to tackle the great problems with which the future executive will have to deal. At worst, it is a reactionary bible for those whose subtle purpose is to divide communities and prevent community action.

Voting will remain useful for some purposes—to record the majority's will in a legislature when negotiation and compromise have failed to persuade a minority, and to elect the legislators and political executives who will serve as surrogates for the people's outrage and confusion. But as our problems mount, it is all too clear that more and more of them cannot be solved by bringing them to a vote. In the short run it may be necessary to outvote the polluters; but for the longer pull they need to be convinced that contributing to pollution is an act against their own interest. It is not enough to declare against the status quo. Change has to be organized in such a way as to include in the changes the devotees of things as they are. It is only a first step to choose sides for and against civil rights; we have to persuade those who, in pursuit of their own free convictions, would deny the freedom of conviction to other citizens.

When I visit the islands and continent to the west of Hawaii,

I notice that Pacific and Asian friends seem instinctively to know what we who have grown up in the Western democracies find so hard to accept. It would not occur to most Chinese to hold a meeting at a rectangular table, forcing the participants to choose sides before they can even sit down. Despite their hierarchical form, the processes of Japanese business seem to leave plenty of room for decisions by consensus. A Samoan board meeting, or a Javanese village council, somehow gets its business done without Robert's *Rules*. In much of the non-Western world, the decision-making proceeds without choosing sides, in ways analogous to a jury or a Quaker meeting, through traditions that encourage men and women to talk out (or decide not to press) their differences—instead of hardening them by clarifying them.

The management of large organization systems will require a great deal of talking and listening, in an effort to take every interest into account and yet emerge with relevant policy decisions and executive action. The world's work will not be tackled by identifying our differences, but by sitting down, preferably at a round table, working hard at the politics of consensus, bringing people together rather than splitting them apart.

The central principle of consensus is that it is possible for people to agree on next steps to be taken, without being able to agree on why they are acting together. In a complex process each interested group has a reason for advocating action. Typically, many of the actions desired can be concerted through negotiation—a Public Executive normally serving as conductor—provided no attempt is made to formulate a concerted philosophy too.

We saw in Chapter 2 that success in managing a web of tensions required a taste for ambiguity. (The many-sidedness

84

of real executive problems suggests a made-up word: "ambi-" means two-sided, so it might better be called a taste for *polyguity*.) If the inside of each organization can be described as a web of tensions, its outside relations—with clients, veto groups, banks, unions, special-interest associations, public agencies, and legislatures—can be seen as a larger tension system, with Public Executives at each switching station trying to bring people together with a view to taking a next step. The prizes go to those who can move toward their subjective human purposes by tolerating a high degree of polyguity in return for a maximum amount of action. That compels the Public Executive to be ethically responsible for his or her own sense of direction. The implications are considered in Chapters 8 and 9.

The Public Executive, mobilizing experts with a view to action, is bound to observe that often the sum of specialized advice is to do nothing cautiously. Anyone with general executive experience has noticed that the most narrowly specialized member of his staff is likely to be the stubbornest staff conservative. Gloom and reluctance are the trademarks of expertise. Hence the executive must always be ready to supply a pinch of unwarranted optimism to the stew of calculated costs and rationalized benefits.

Just at present the expert predictions of disaster center on the uncontrolled increase in population and the degradation of the environment. (The demographers may be compensating for past error—the Census Bureau in 1945 guessed that the United States would reach a population of 167 million by 1995, then we rocketed past that figure in the mid-1950s.) The dangers of overpopulation are very real, and do not need to be embroidered with straight-line projections which depend for their validity on the assumption that the probable countervailing trends will not countervail. The environmentalists are likewise prone to play with long-range forecasts, in which the gloomiest of alternative futures emerge as the most probable.

There is a contribution to be made by professional gloom, if it moves people-in-general to insist on changing the future by acting in the present. But prophecies of disaster do not usually move people to action. Cassandra was always right, but Apollo easily arranged for her to be always ineffective. We know the potential danger of nuclear weapons, but hardly anybody builds a fallout shelter in his garden. A mayor has difficulty coalescing the urban electorate around a charge that there is no place to park downtown. Yet he can sometimes develop political and financial support for a plan to build municipal parking garages. What moves people to action is more hope than fear, not just a vision of how bad things might become, but a vision of how things might be improved.

This is where the Public Executive comes in. It is his professional obligation to supply the unwarranted optimism that sets the man of action off from the well-documented advisory prophet of doom. His contribution to any organization system is to remember that the ethical content of planning need not be limited to a lugubrious comparison in which the future always seems less attractive than the present. As Teilhard de Chardin emphasized (perhaps this is the reason for his latter-day popularity), man is not to be a passive witness but a participant in the evolutionary process.

Major departures in public policy—for good *and* for ill—are more frequently the product of some executive's unwarranted optimism than of careful expert staff work. In early 1943 Harry Hopkins, who was President Franklin Roosevelt's closest confidant, was helping the President prepare his State of the Union Message. Targets for war production were to be set in the speech, and Hopkins cited a report from a panel of experts that the United States economy, by straining every nerve, could produce 25,000 military aircraft the following year. Twenty-five thousand doesn't sound like enough, the President said to Hopkins; let's double it and add ten. The aircraft industry did not quite meet the Roosevelt target of 60,000 planes that year. But spurred by a leader's act of leadership, it did turn out 49,000 planes, almost double what the experts had said was possible.

Many of the inspired initiatives in our international relations have been similarly based more on a leader's ethical hunch than on rational analysis before the fact. (Again, this does not guarantee a "good" initiative; some leaders' hunches have proved very bad for mankind.) I once had occasion to ask Jean Monnet, the father of the Schuman Plan for a European Coal-Steel Authority, about the origins of that imaginative and successful enterprise. "I certainly didn't consult any experts on coal and steel," he said. "They would have told me it was impossible." President Kennedy's 1961 decision to set a 1969 deadline for man on the Moon; President Eisenhower's calls for "open skies" and "atoms for peace"; Secretary of State George Marshall's Harvard speech which led to the European Recovery Program; and President Truman's "Point Four" proposal to extend technical aid to the world's less developed nations, all were exercises in optimism unwarranted by the then available expert advice. In each case the major planning effort followed, and did not precede, the public-policy initiative. I attended the first interdepartmental meeting to carry "Point Four" into action. Around a long table in the State Department sat all the government's ranking experts on technical aid to less developed countries; none had known ahead of time that the President would include "Point Four" in his

Inaugural Address a few days before. The chairman, Assistant Secretary of State Willard Thorp, slowly looked around the gathering. "Well, gentlemen," he said at last, "what do you suppose the President meant?"

If planning is improvisation on a general sense of direction, then the executive leader's primary task is to establish, maintain, advertise, and continuously amend a sense of direction that his colleagues in complexity can share. The conviction that the goals he helps set are possible of achievement is an indispensable part of his psyche. His is the optimism of the doer, unwarranted by the experience of others but justified by his own determination to organize a future with a difference. Emerson said it: "Nothing great was ever achieved without enthusiasm."

Chapter 7

The Exhilaration of Choice

Guess if you can,
Choose if you dare.
—*Pierre Corneille*

The future executive will be brainy, low-key, collegial, optimistic, and one thing more—he will positively enjoy complexity and constant change.

People who shy away from executive work often say they feel imprisoned by the multiplicity of options and the ambiguities of jurisdiction which are the stuff of large-scale organization systems. The effective executive, on the other hand, is likely to be a person who delights in the chance to choose the best path according to his own lights. For the Public Executive, the "feel" of administration is the exhilaration of choice.

At Expo 67 in Montreal, the tasteful exhibit from Czecho-slovakia attracted the most attention, and its outstanding fea-ture was a remarkable film about the selection of options in motion. The screenplay starts conventionally enough: The day is warm; a beautiful girl, scantily clad, is ironing in her apartment. By some series of accidents I cannot remember, she goes out into the hall wearing nothing but a towel, and the door slams behind her. Of course she doesn't have her key, and she is distraught as she imagines her iron, still on, burning the fabric and setting the apartment house afire. She knocks on the door of the apartment next door; a man emerges. He, too, has a problem: knowing that his wife will be back in a moment, should he invite the nearly naked girl into his apart-ment while he tries to help her?

Suddenly the movie stops, the house lights go on, and a real-life man appears through a trap door on the stage in front of the darkened screen. The man is the actor we have just been watching on the screen. "Stop the movie!" he cries, and turns to the audience. "What shall I do now?" He explains that each member of the audience has a console at his side, and can vote whether he should invite the toweled blonde into his apartment or slam the door in her face. The audience votes, chivalry wins by a narrow margin, the house lights go off and the movie reappears, pursuing the action that follows from the option we have selected. The wife returns, draws the obvious conclusion, and leaves her man; there is still an iron presum-ably setting the whole building on fire; it is not long before another excruciating choice presents itself. Again the movie stops, the trap door opens, the girl actress this time appears in the flesh (though properly clothed according to Eastern

European standards) and asks the audience for a decision. Evidently the movie maker had a whole scenario worked out for each option, no matter which fork in the road each audience elected each time the movie was shown. After a hilarious hour, with more audience participation than I have ever seen in a movie house, the ambiguities are resolved in an ironic O. Henry finish.

The enormous popularity of this film at Expo 67 is easily explained: the ethical dilemmas it presented were transmuted from a celluloid image to the reasoning conscience of each member of the audience. Instead of observing other people's dilemmas, the dilemmas suddenly became ours.

The central function of the executive is to choose among alternative action options as he goes along—not just for himself but for others, too. The more responsibility he carries, the harder the dilemmas he faces: if they were not hard, they would not reach him for resolution. In Washington one observes that issues reaching the President or even the Secretary of State are no longer rational choices. My rule of thumb in the State Department was that if an answer could rationally be given a 51-to-49 chance of being "right," the problem could be settled by brokerage among the bureaus without bothering the Cabinet level. By the time an issue gets to the ultimate political executives, it has been proved insoluble by logic and reason; the chief ingredients in high policy are gut feelings and ethical hunch.

Even Robert McNamara, who as Secretary of Defense tried so hard to apply reason to policy, concluded that "Management is, in the end, the most creative of all the arts, for its medium is human talent itself." Like painting or sculpture or dance, the management of social complexity cannot be taught by rote, but it can be learned by example and inspiration and unremitting practice. What Michel de Montaigne said of the arts and sciences is doubly true of the qualities of executive leadership: they are not cast in a mold, but are formed and perfected by degrees, by frequent handling and polishing, as bears leisurely lick their cubs into form.

What makes the executive's life exciting is that the choices he makes, or helps make, are *in motion*. It used to be said of the good executive that he was "driving"; a more accurate word would now be "steering." The momentum is already built in—the executive's task is to give it direction, to cause the momentum to serve a subjective human purpose by channeling it in a system managed by human beings and not by blind fate.

Because I used to race sailboats in my youth, I have often thought the feel of executive responsibility analogous to the feel of a small boat in competition. The skipper must know well what his craft will and won't do, and what his crew can handle, especially in emergencies. He has to have done his homework—looked up the timing and force and direction of the tides and currents that afternoon, listened to the weather forecast, studied wind-shift tactics and the racing rules. He must know as much as possible about the psychology of the other skippers and the performance of their boats—some faster in light airs, some able to point higher on a windward beat, some especially swift on a spinnaker run. With all these data stored for instant retrieval, he must analyze a constantly moving situation, in which the air, the water, the other boats, and his own boat are continuously changing their relations to one another. And then he makes decisions—several major "policy" decisions per minute if the class is large and the competition keen. Win or lose, he is unlikely to be bored.

A year after the British electorate had retired him as Chancellor of the Exchequer in a Labour Government, Roy Jenkins proposed skiing as the best way to describe the exhilaration of choice in motion. He contrasted private writing and public responsibility:

A hard period of writing is like a walk up a steep mountainside. There is no natural momentum behind one. It all has to be self-generated. . . . [But the writer] can mostly control his own pace, and his intermediate failures are private rather than public. There are no onlookers to mock his periods of ineffective immobility.

Ministerial work, on the other hand, is much more like skiing down a slalom course. The momentum is all on one's side, provided it can be controlled. There is little difficulty about generating the will to proceed. There is a rapid and relentless movement from one event to another . . . each event comes up with such rapidity that there is relatively little danger of falling through hesitation or over-anxiety. They have to be taken as they come, on the run; and a lot of things are better done this way.

Neither analogy is very close. The object of executive work is usually not to win a race but to make cooperation work. And the slalom image would be better if at each gate the skier were presented with two or three alternative ways to proceed. But both images convey the essential sense of motion. Because the whole environment of administration is constantly in motion, nobody can quite know just how the situation looks to an individual executive except the executive himself. Within the limits of relevance, therefore, he must choose his own path, and live with the consequences.

To some, the obligation to choose too fast and too often will seem a burden, a cause for complaint and a reason for frustration. But to those who have the stuff to be our future executives, the momentum will carry its own excitement, and the opportunity to participate in destiny decisions will more than repay the days of committee-sitting and the nights of reading and writing.

For many Public Executives, perhaps most, the exhilaration of choice is the primary reward for service and the chief ingredient in "morale." But that feeling of joy in getting things done by getting decisions made has to be generated from within—for the nature of modern leadership is that the leadership doesn't show. To maximize his own morale, the Public Executive has to learn to *internalize credit* for what he does.

For a few executives, especially those in top positions, public notice and even approbation are available as inducements to develop the skills and carry the ethical burdens that go with their function in society. (There is of course the offsetting risk of public opprobrium. For a time a new recruit to the ranks of Public Executives may feel that the choices he makes are so complicated, and the criteria of his success so obscure, that it is almost impossible for outsiders to judge his performance on the job. The probability is indeed diminishing of any interested public's being able to understand what the decision was about or what his part in it was. Yet this does not necessarily make life safer for the Public Executive. For when a judgment *is* rendered, the public's ignorance, combined with its ultimate power, may render the verdict more unfair than it might have been in simpler times or more static societies.) For most Public Executives, however, their very function precludes their taking credit for the most important things they do. The staff man who writes a policy speech for the President; the analyst whose staff work enables his boss to keep the firm in the black; the personnel manager who keeps a crack designer from quitting in disgust, and thus ensures better design work on next year's car; the general counsel who drafts a major piece of legislation (of which a Senator is said to be the "author" because he introduces it); the American ambassador who thinks up a useful initiative, and then persuades a foreign colleague to float it publicly—none of these can take credit for their work without interfering with the desired results. The mark of a good colleague is that he not hog the credit for collective accomplishment, and the mark of a good staff man that the person functionally responsible for a decision not be deprived of the credit for making it.

While I worked in the State Department, I signed or uttered hundreds of memos, policy cables, speeches, and articles which were the work of others. Pretending they were mine made them mine—neither accolades nor backlash from the affected publics fell out on my analysts or ghost writers. But the colleagues who wrote my stuff had to learn the art of taking credit vicariously—and privately.

Similarly on several occasions I contributed major chunks of thinking and writing to President Kennedy's statements and foreign-policy speeches. In the nature of things, the Kennedy biographer who served as the President's chief writer later attributed to his own initiative ideas that thus originated in other parts of the Federal bureaucracy. The President did not live to say what he himself remembered, but it is altogether probable that he would have considered that the ideas in his policy speeches were his own; wherever originated, he had made them his own by understanding them and taking public responsibility for making them Presidential policy.

President Kennedy was acutely conscious of where credit and blame might fall. On one occasion, after we had worked out in his office a complicated scheme for handling some foreign-policy issue, he sent us back to our offices with a cheerful parting shot. "I hope this plan works," said the President of the United States. "If it does, it will be another White House success. If it doesn't, it will be another State Department failure." But I was in the Cabinet Room the day it became clear that the Bay of Pigs invasion was a fiasco; President Kennedy promptly took full responsibility for the mistake.

Of course there are many kinds of social rewards for executive work short of applause from the general public. Usually a few people know the situation well, and their private congratulations count for much. The Central Intelligence Agency operative or the FBI undercover man, who may not even be able to tell their wives what they are doing, know that people in their own organization whose opinion they value are aware of their assignments and recording their triumphs.

Nevertheless, most of the credit for accomplishment—and most of the blame for failure, too—is internalized. I learned in the diplomatic service to derive active pleasure from reflecting on my part in defusing several peace-and-security crises and averting several near-wars, without boasting to anyone outside my immediate family. The capacity to internalize the credit for what you do is certainly an acquired skill, unnatural to the human psyche. An executive needs to acquire it early, for the nature of modern leadership is that it doesn't show— and especially that it doesn't show off.

Part Three

Purposes

Chapter 8

Executive Feet to the Fire

If you would not be known to do anything, never do it.
—*Ralph Waldo Emerson*

During the time when Charles Van Doren was pretending to be an intellectual giant on a rigged TV quiz show, and before he was caught in the act, he and his legitimately famous father, Mark Van Doren, were chosen as "The Father-and-Son Team of the Year" by the National Father's Day Committee. The grateful remarks that father and son made in accepting the award, read through the hindsight of Charles' later confession that his brilliance was a hoax, take on the quality of prophetic wisdom.

Father was the first to speak. Our later knowledge leaves his words untarnished:

I claim no credit for [Charles'] being what he is . . . people make their own intellectual and moral characters. If he was helped in making his by me . . . it was he who decided to accept the help. The decision in such matters is finally with ourselves. To say that responsibility begins at home should mean, I think, that it begins— and ends, too—in the individual. Sooner or later he must help himself. There are no alibis.

Charles Van Doren then rose to accept his public's accolade, and spoke of his father.

. . . He has been able to move me, to laughter and to tears, for as long as I can remember.

Both in public and in private—and that's of the greatest importance. For my father has been, to me, both a public and a private man. Oh, perhaps not as public a man as I have become recently. We have laughed about this, he and I. . . .

But, my experience has reminded me of something that he taught me—not consciously, I'm sure, but as an example. For the extraordinary thing about my father is that his public face and his private face have been the same. He has been the same man to the world as he has been to his family. And that is harder than it sounds. It is the very definition of integrity, I suppose.

If a line cannot be drawn between "public" and "private" on the basis of ownership but only on the basis of interest and utility and purpose, it follows that the Public Executive is marked not by his *affiliation* with a public agency but by his *acceptance* of the public responsibility he carries, whatever the character of the organization in which he carries it. And if the ultimate judgment about the quality of an executive's "public" actions can be made only by people-in-general, the ultimate court is the public's outrage. Therefore the best way to keep the Public Executives' feet to the fire is to make sure that the decisions in which they participate, and the identity of the participants, are publicly known. The best antidote to irresponsibility is openness.

This is a hard doctrine. It means that the quality of public ethics in our time and place rests in the first instance on the moral sensitivity, the political antennae, and the internalized standards of hundreds of thousands of Public Executives in thousands of public and "private" organizations. Each of these individuals is already carrying around a wide assortment of tugs and pulls on his conscience—family ties, loyalty to many organizations (neighborhood, church, commune, volunteer agencies, schools, professional associations, as well as "the job"), professional ethics, personal ambition, personal health, and his own convictions about life styles. Now we add to this already complex moral burden an elusive responsibility to an often apathetic general public. And we say that in modern society the public interest must be first defined for each person by that person, for each situation in that situation.

The concept of the public interest has been analyzed so much by writers and teachers that I am reluctant to add another page to the literature. But I observe that in facing practical problems many people still think there must be some formula, some overriding principle, some universal criterion of judgment and action which is objective and ascertainable: "Didn't he *know* that what he did was against the public interest?" Yet there is no ethical realm, let alone a book about ethics, from which the individual faced with complex judgments can pluck the answers to the questions with which he faces himself. And paradoxically, the more complex things become, the more personal the ethical judgments have to be. Cultural pluralism, diffusion of power, and horizontalness of decision-making require us to think of the public interest not as a code of ethics for the world, or for the nation, or even for a single organization, but as a nontransferable way of thinking developed by each Public Executive for his or her own use.

In practice this way of thinking is compounded of the perceived standards of others, molded to fit one's own experience in trying to apply those standards to real-life problems. We start by deriving our "deep-down" feelings about public responsibility from our early environment—from family and school and church, from the organizations with which we are perforce associated, from heroes and friends and villains and enemies. Then as we gain more experience, we develop our personal notions from the injustices we see practiced or find we are practicing ourselves, from the examples we see of social and antisocial behavior, from reading and listening, from experimenting with personal leadership. After a while, each person's ethical system is at least a little different from anyone else's. (The disagreements we call politics; if they are violent, we call them revolutions.)

As in the evolution of law, precedent and precept are some help. An analysis of the exercise of public responsibility in some historical situation, where we now think we know most of the relevant facts, may aid in solving tomorrow's similar (but never identical) problems for ourselves; hence the heavy use of "case method" teaching in law schools, business schools, and schools of public affairs and administration.

Wise sayings from Mencius and Aristotle, the Bible and the Founding Fathers, not to mention our own parents, may likewise be useful but hardly controlling; with a little help from a concordance of the Bible or Bartlett's *Familiar Quotations,* it is all too easy to find some pseudo-scriptural basis for whatever one really wants to do. New principles do not need to be written, by the Public Executive or his ghost writer; they all seem to have been uttered already by Old Testament prophets, Chinese and Indian sages, the teachers and saviors of the world's great religions, the ancient Greeks and the early Christians. But they do not of course provide much guidance on what to do next—how to cope with riots and poverty and discrimination, whether to deploy an ABM system or build another office building, what to do and who should do it in Berkeley and Newark and Biafra and Vietnam. They are even less helpful in deciding how to chair a committee meeting or whether to hire Miss Peckensniff. Some of our forefathers' wisdom may even be part of the problem. Pollution, urban decay, and the weapons of frightfulness are pretty directly traceable to the Age of Enlightenment.

Each ethically independent executive thus has to apply to the reality around him the notions about procedure which he has gleaned from his own study and experience. But the most conspicuous component of that reality is the presence of other ethically independent individuals who are applying *their* differing criteria to *his* behavior. This requires him to develop judgments about the motivations of the publics in whose interests he presumes to act, those same publics which will ultimately judge whether he measures up to a minimum standard of public responsibility for his time, place, and function.

In these circumstances a written code of ethics can never be comprehensive enough or subtle enough to be a satisfactory guide to personal behavior as a Public Executive. Louis Hector, a lawyer who served on the Civil Aeronautics Board, put it succinctly: general prescriptions, whether in the form of do's or don't's, are bound to be "so general as to be useless or so specific as to be unworkable."

Lacking an affirmative code of ethics, I developed while I was working in the Federal Government a key question to ask myself just before getting committed to a line of action. The question was designed to reflect *both* the judgment which people-in-general might later make on my behavior *and* my own reaction in the face of that judgment. The question still seems to me well designed to compel me to project my own feelings in the dramatic rehearsal of imagined public scrutiny of my actions, and the procedures by which they are decided.

The question is not "Will I be criticized?" If I am operating in the area of public responsibility, the answer to that question is quite likely to be "Yes." The (to me) illuminating question is this:

"If this action is held up to public scrutiny, will I still feel that it is what I should have done, and how I should have done it?"

If those involved had asked themselves this question and answered it honestly, most of the famous instances of public corruption which enliven and debase our political history might never have happened.

Sometimes the issues are large—incestuous relations between the military services and their contractors, major diversions of public monies to private purposes. Teapot Dome and Dixon-Yates come readily to mind. But the human drama and pathos are not in the cases of international profiteering, but in ethically opaque behavior by upright men so confused by public complexity that the distinction between right and wrong gets blurred along with the line between "public" and "private."

If General Harry Vaughan in the Truman White House had asked himself whether the transaction depended for its acceptability on its not becoming public, he would never have accepted the deep-freeze that helped defeat the Democrats in 1952. If Sherman Adams in the Eisenhower White House had not considered his relations with Bernard Goldfine an untouchable private affair, he surely would not have stained his image of New England rectitude by accepting the gift of a vicuna coat. When Bobby Baker was trading Senatorial influence for business opportunities, did he think his powerful sponsorship made him invisible? When Harold Talbott wrote endorsements for his private management firm, using his official stationery as Secretary of the Air Force, only the public outcry and his consequent dismissal seemed to illuminate for him the ethical issue involved. Supreme Court Justice Abe Fortas, whose reputation as a lawyer was built by purveying sound and sensitive advice to clients operating in the no-man's land of public/private enterprise, could not have banked a fee from a stock manipulator if he had asked himself the "will I still feel" question.

There have been efforts, notable more for courage than for workability, to pass quantitative rules about the private relations of public servants. In Washington, for example, the issue of what gifts, if any, a government official should accept is a chronic source of private trouble and public entertainment. Senator Paul Douglas of Illinois, an economist, tried to draw the line at gifts worth $2.50. "Some of my friends humorously suggest that this rule shows that I have little faith in my own ability to withstand temptation," Douglas said in a Harvard lecture. "They say apparently I can resist the allure of a $2.49 present, but not of one worth $2.51. I am willing to accept and indeed smile at these gibes. With all its borderline difficulties, the rule has helped keep me from major involvements and it has done so with a minimum of spiritual wear and tear." Michael DiSalle, former Governor of Ohio, who earlier headed the Office of Price Administration, ordered employees of OPA not to accept as a gift anything that could not be consumed in twenty-four hours. I recall a stimulating evening when a group of young civil servants tried to apply this rule

105

to the gifts their bosses were receiving. A Smithfield ham was clearly within bounds—though one man in the Bureau of Internal Revenue had testified to a Congressional committee that he drew the line at a twelve-pound ham. It was not so clear whether, if you had a large enough circle of thirsty friends, it would be within the DiSalle doctrine to accept a case of Scotch.

Perhaps the limiting case of ethical opacity was recorded shortly before an Assistant Attorney General, T. Lamar Caudle, drew a jail sentence for corruption in a former job as United States District Attorney in North Carolina. Caudle, according to Senator Douglas, "testified that he used to leave the side window of his automobile open when he parked it, and that he was always surprised by the wide variety of presents which were generously and anonymously thrown into the back seat by unknown admirers and friends."

Some of Washington's most vivid illustrations of private confusions about public ethics occur at each change of Administration, when those new Presidential appointees who happen to be rich are pressed to sell their stock in private enterprises that do business with the government. The Senators who interview the nominees do not really think a rich businessman is motivated by profit to take a government job. But if a man is going to manage public monies, he must not be seen to stand too close to the fuzzy line between "public" and "private." In January 1953, General Motors President Charles E. Wilson was nominated as Secretary of Defense. After two long days of public hearings in which Senators were urging the nominee to get rid of his very large GM stock holdings, Wilson made a revealing comment. "The thing that perhaps I overlooked myself," he mused, "was that not only did I have to operate honestly and fairly without prejudice, but all the people should also think that that was the way I was operating, and that part of it I did not quite appraise." The Senators were stunned. How does a man get to be sixty-two years old and president of the world's largest corporation without having "quite appraised" the Biblical admonition to avoid not only evil but the appearance of evil?

"If this action is held up to public scrutiny, will I still feel that it is what I should have done, and how I should have done it?" If a TV cameraman had been taking pictures at My Lai that day, would Lieutenant William Calley have killed those Vietnamese civilians huddled in the ditch? War diffuses the responsibility for life-and-death decisions, and the central ethical question left by Calley's trial—Calley was guilty of the murders, but who was *responsible*—was never resolved. In part Calley has to be adjudged responsible. In the field the local commander has considerable discretion.

The "will I still feel" question is intentionally two-edged. It is designed to prevent me (and anybody else who cares to use it) from playing God, taking the full ethical responsibility for a judgment which can ultimately be validated only by some relevant public. But it is also designed to avoid the equal and opposite danger: that an action about which I have doubts becomes all right if others—my colleagues in an organization, my professional peers, my family, my friends and neighbors— can be counted on not to object. Judging your actions by what others would think is as risky as judging them by what you alone think. William Attwood reported in *Look* on "an extreme and ironic case of neo-moral conformity in Colorado, where a man who did *not* chisel on his income tax boasted that he did. To be well regarded by his friends, he pretended to be doing what he assumed the group considered smart." The case of young Charles Van Doren, who cheated to make a TV quiz program successful, was only an especially dramatic instance of a person who thought he could transplant organizational ethics wholesale, without marrying them to a public responsibility concept of his own. In another famous instance of the corruptive power of the mass media, Sam Snead found on the fourteenth hole of a televised golf tournament that he had one extra club in his bag and was therefore automatically disqualified. Instead of saying so forthwith, Snead finished out the match, but contrived to putt so badly that he lost. The show must go on, he must have felt, and the National Broadcasting Company thought so too: in full knowledge of Snead's unusual way of disqualifying himself, the network later aired the match without warning the television audience that Snead had deliberately "taken a dive" during the last few holes.

People caught in ethical thickets such as these are often heard to blame their troubles on the System—the corruption of the mass media or the oppressive weight of the institution they serve. Thus a TV producer who is a little ashamed of his moral responsibility for loading the airwaves with a half-dozen crime stories a week will tell you that the public insists on it, or that the advertisers make him do it. But what makes a modern Public Executive free (the military are only partly an exception) is precisely his ability to go and do something else. If he does not go and do something else, the rest of us have the right to presume that his moral discomfort is offset by the more tangible comforts of his position. He cannot claim to be *both* ashamed *and* oppressed—for that would relieve him of the private responsibility for his public actions which is, as Mark and Charles Van Doren agreed, the very definition of integrity.

The first line of defense against antipublic actions by Public Executives is to develop their own moral sensitivities. The second line of defense is public outrage. Both grow best in the open.

The 1960s in America saw the greening of public outrage, combined with a growing insistence that decisions on public policy be more openly arrived at. The war in Vietnam was a particularly good subject for healthy indignation: not only did it clearly become a costly, inconclusive, and embarrassingly unilateral adventure, but the process by which President Johnson committed the nation and the Senate to combat on the Asian mainland struck many people as stealthy. During this same period students and many others, not all of them young, were experimenting with public outrage directed at many other targets—racial discrimination, police tactics, restraints on free speech, censorship of the press, poverty, the sluggishness of educational reform, the degradation of the environment, the invasion of privacy, antiballistic missile systems, incompetent judges, unsafe automobiles, supersonic planes, price gouging, urban sprawl and ugliness.

Much public outrage has taken the form of organized protest by petition, march, and mass visitation, shading over into sit-ins, forcible restraint (usually of Public Executives), vandalism, and violence. The most impressive new life style in America is not the informality of dress, the public surfacing of sex, or the eighteenth-century hair length, but the proclivity of Americans to demonstrate in public when aroused. This has long been a natural mode of action for delegates to political conventions and students living in college dormitories. But now the street rally and the mass visitation are widely used by all kinds of people in every part of the political spectrum.

Yet the staying power of spontaneous citizen protest is not impressive. An especially outrageous public action (the unanticipated invasion of Cambodia, the premature use of police on campus) can trigger a vigorous, even violent reaction for a few hours or a few days; but the half-life of popular indignation is short. Citizen demonstrations are effective in stopping or delaying actions by Public Executives, but the sustained effort required to get something new started or (a fortiori) finished was generally beyond the capacity of citizen and student protest in the 1960s.

Staying power requires a wide consensus among the protesters on a minimum where-are-we-trying-to-go doctrine. The Communists did as well as they did in Europe and Asia because they organized in the service of an "inevitable" history: they had a Manifesto and a Book, and in Lenin and Mao Tsetung they found brilliant tacticians who were good at adapting antique doctrines to fit the tactical requirements of the struggle for power. The radical leadership of "the movement" during the 1960s lacked a doctrine to glue together the pluralistic energy unleashed by a variety of frustrations in a dozen cities and on a hundred campuses. Some were not even sure they wanted to establish new institutions in place of the old, suspecting that human institutions as such are irremediable; there has been more than a little of Robinson Crusoe in the recent rhetoric of revolt. But if a revolutionary leader distrusts organization and is allergic to power, he is unlikely to seize power or organize to hang onto it.

This skepticism of doctrine, combined with hostility to organized power, led some revolutionary leaders to be openly scornful of "causes." To generate some action, to shake things up, became for some an end in itself. On university campuses especially, the most militant leaders of mini-revolutions have tended to narrow their substantive targets, and move as quickly as possible toward procedural issues to widen immediate support for "action." They found that they could start with some substantive issue like ROTC or the Columbia University gymnasium or the right to use a "people's park," but to get a large excited crowd into the streets they had to shift the focus as rapidly as possible to a question of procedure—a failure of due process, "cops on campus," or whatever. Analyzing the "events of May" 1968 at the Sorbonne in Paris, Raymond Aron described in a capsule the pattern of U.S. campus disruption: ". . . teachers and students, divided among themselves on most subjects, find a factitious unity in opposing power and the police. If a few students want to bring on repressive measures by the civil authorities, nobody can prevent them from doing so. . . . This leads to the 'police brutality' which the doctrinaires of violence both desire and denounce."

If a substantive issue is useful only as a trigger, and is merely the tactical symbol of a System which is rotten to the core, the issue itself does not require careful research or the exhaustion of conventional remedies. When the national Students for a Democratic Society selected the Reserve Officers Training Corps as a prime target on all American campuses, that was a signal that campus disruption, not a drastic reduction of the military influence in America, was their central purpose. On campus after campus the antiwar movement was lured away from the juiciest and most relevant targets—the national military-industrial complex, the size of the military budget, the continuation of the war in Vietnam—and concentrated instead on tweaking the local military toe called ROTC. The quality of the debate even on that subject was not high: ROTC was seen as a means to confrontation, not as a subject in itself. The confrontations were often achieved, but they left little residue. Meanwhile, the initiative on military spending, on the Defense Department's contractual arrangements, and even on troop withdrawal from Vietnam was left with the national Administration.

On subjects other than war and peace, however, the spasm

111

of protest in the sixties left behind the beginnings of some permanent machinery for mobilizing and aiming the public outrage. Civil rights organizations grew out of racial protest, and remained to litigate in the courts and lobby in the legislatures. Rioting in the cities left a strengthened Urban League and an Urban Coalition. Housewives' increasingly vocal objections to being cheated pushed the Federal and some state governments into setting up consumer advocates, partly to do battle with the many other interests already encamped within the bureaucratic walls. Philanthropists gave money to organizations designed to improve the quality and targeting of outrage—though the fear of government regulation has latterly constrained their courage. Legislatures, realizing they had delegated more than they intended of their real power to mayors and governors and Presidents, brushed up on their right of inquiry, always a powerful instrument in mobilizing public outrage and enhancing their bargaining power with the executive branch of government.

The movement with the most charisma, and potentially the most staying power, has been that associated with the name of Ralph Nader. A young law student gets interested in highway safety. He concludes that part of the trouble is the way the auto makers build autos. He sets forth on a lonely crusade against General Motors. He publishes a book, *Unsafe at Any Speed*, which catches the public fancy. General Motors collaborates, by putting detectives on his trail. He sues General Motors, and collects a large sum, which he invests in establishing a Center for Responsive Law in Washington. Students and young lawyers flock to join or emulate him. And he finds he has created a new kind of institution, the public-interest law firm backed up by a public-interest research group, to do the homework required to keep the Public Executives in private corporations and government agencies aware of their public responsibilities.

Nader proved something of far-reaching importance—that it takes energy, brains, and careful research to keep Public Executives honest and alert, but it does not require vast resources or very large institutions. He himself would doubtless agree that the monitoring service will work best if its power, too, is diffused: a thousand Naders scattered around the country would be far more effective than a "Nader Organization" a thousand times the size of his relatively small and impressively helter-skelter Center.

The other public-outrage-mobilizing service that shows real signs of life as of 1971 is the environmental movement. Concern about the quality of air and water, the condition of the land and the degradation of the oceans, the mercury in the fish and the cyclamates in the artificial sugar, the phosphates in the detergents and the lead in the gasoline, the dangers of the colored dyes in our tissues and the chemicals in our bug sprays, the general feeling that we are about to be overwhelmed by undisposable waste and unmanageable numbers of babies, has grown so fast that some citizens in every community have appointed themselves to cry havoc. The volunteers are often not the most careful researchers or the most effective spokesmen. But in league with university scientists, disgruntled public servants, old conservationists, and young professionals bored with their normal career outlook but excited by the coming battles over ecology, they have enormously enhanced the public awareness of environmental dangers.

Except in extreme cases, the executives in government agencies and large corporations and nonprofit agencies would not even hear about the public's present or prospective outrage if it were not reported, and in some instances generated, by newspapers, TV, and radio. If exposure is so important in preventing actions that are thoughtless of the public interest or deliberately designed to bypass it, the managers of the communications media have a crucial role to play in this multilateral system of checks and balances. This means that the media managers, too, are Public Executives, and like others of their breed are responsible to no one or everyone. Who, then, checks the checkers?

Newspaper editors and TV-radio station managers are often heard in passionate defense of their freedom to publish according to their own lights, without prior restraint by the government's Public Executives. This freedom, like other freedoms enjoyed by large organizations affected with the public interest, is inherently constrained by the acceptability of its exercise to people-in-general. During the moral crisis produced by Charles Van Doren's revelation that he was giving memorized answers to prearranged questions on national television, the network executives made their accountability explicit. "It is our responsibility," said NBC's Robert Kintner, "to make sure that these programs will be honestly conducted, so that the public can have confidence in all the programs it watches." Frank Stanton of CBS was on the same wavelength: "We are responsible for what appears on CBS. We accept that responsibility. . . . We are only obligated to do one thing and that is to be responsible to the American people."

The American people can no more leave the use of their airwaves to the unreviewed judgment of Public Executives in the networks than they can leave stream pollution to the unreviewed judgment of Public Executives in private industrial firms. A Federal agency therefore licenses TV and radio transmissions—though this power has not been used effectively to

114

deter cultural pollution of the airwaves. For newspapers, however, there is no comparable licensing service on behalf of people-in-general. If a barber wants to cut my hair, he has to have a permit; if a newspaperman wants to cut my throat, all he needs is a typewriter and some white space in tomorrow's edition.

The constitutional battle over the Pentagon Papers in 1971 emphasized how heavy and how unreviewed is the obligation of a newspaper's Public Executives to decide what they are going to print and when. The Attorney General was frustrated in three Federal courts on the issue of "prior restraint" of the publication of Top Secret government documents, however procured. By their actions the courts, including the United States Supreme Court, said in effect that it is up to the editors to decide what is fit to print; the government can review that judgment after the fact but not before.

The judgment of editors is a sometime thing; consistency over time is hard enough for an individual, and harder yet for an institution whose personnel naturally changes. In December 1962, the *New York Times* carried an editorial attacking the *Saturday Evening Post* for revealing actions of the National Security Council during the Cuban crisis six weeks before. The *Times* had itself voluntarily withheld information it had at the time, to avoid scooping President Kennedy on the announcement that Soviet missiles were present in Cuba. (The *Times* also knew more about Bay of Pigs planning, earlier in the game, than it revealed in its news columns.) In an editorial entitled "Breach of Security," the *Times'* judgment on the *Saturday Evening Post*'s judgment was scornful: "How can advisers to the President be expected to give advice freely and easily and at all times honestly and with complete integrity if

115

they have to worry about what their arguments will look like in print a few weeks hence?"

Eight and a half years and 45,000 American deaths later, the *New York Times* had concluded that it was all right to publish Top Secret documents if a three-year period had elapsed between confidential advice to the President and national publication by the *Times*. My own instinct is more favorable to the *Times'* more recent interpretation of its public responsibility. Perhaps it would sharpen the judgments and make the Presidential advice more honest if all the advisers had to pass their advice through that piece of litmus paper: "How will I feel if this advice is later held up to public scrutiny?" Would all of LBJ's advisers have said just the same things in their memoranda if they had been asking themselves: "Do I want the American people to know that I was pushing escalation in the guise of tit-for-tat retaliation, at a moment when the President was beating his electoral opponent about the ears for wanting to enlarge the war on the Asian mainland?"

The embattled Public Executives at the *New York Times* were more self-conscious about their own position than were some of their more uncritical supporters. "Who elected the *New York Times*?" somebody must have asked in the office when the storm broke over the Pentagon Papers, because for several days the editorial page, James Reston's column, and Max Frankel's interpretative correspondence from Washington used that identical question as a foil for arguing that the *Times* was responsible to people-in-general, and was exercising that responsibility the best it knew how. The *Times'* passion about the war in Vietnam had prevailed over its earlier reasoning about the self-restraint of the press. As Reston had said in another connection two years before, "It is a time of strong passion and weak reason."

116

Executive Feet to the Fire

Who, then, guards the guardians? In the case of the newspapers especially, there is a strong case for a forum in which the Public Executives of the media have to sit down from time to time with the Public Executives from government, "private business," the universities, and other major structures of each community to face the uninhibited criticism of colleagues and justify the unreviewed decisions they make pursuant to their concept of what is good for people-in-general. In Honolulu the University of Hawaii took the initiative to set up a Community-Media Council to experiment with the idea that the quality of the public dialogue can be improved by getting some of the key Public Executives in town to meet once every three or four weeks with the editors of the two main newspapers and the four main television-radio channels. In the absence of some such device, the situation is essentially unfair: the Public Executives in government are responsible to people-in-general through a legislature, the Public Executives in private enterprise are responsible to people-in-general through the communications media, the electronic media are in some sense responsible to the Federal Communications Commission; but the newspapers are responsible in some sense to themselves.

If public ethics are in the hearts and minds of individual Public Executives, and if the ultimate court of appeal from their judgments is some surrogate for people-in-general, it follows that the procedure for making public-policy decisions should be as open as possible. How open is possible—without destroying the basis for cooperation and community?

The value of openness is quickly established. Anybody watching the working of government must be struck by the observation that the most controversial programs tend to be those which generate the least scandal and corruption. The

117

reason is that a program constantly under fire, needing constantly to expose itself by replying to charges or defending its jurisdiction, is so exposed to public scrutiny that for its Public Executives honesty is not only the best policy but the only available option. In Washington it is no accident that matters which frequently get to the White House are so often better handled than those which do not. The Housing Agency worked off in a corner by itself for years, dealing directly with the housing industry and developing an intricate network of corruption which seemed to the Public Executives involved to be the natural order of things until Congress discovered large private profits being made at the public's expense. The foreign-aid program, on the other hand, spent more than fifty billion dollars before scandal began to appear around the edges. In its first decade so many departments and agencies were fighting for the right to manage chunks of the foreign-aid program that the program was the subject of monthly, sometimes even weekly, concern to the President, the Congress, the newspapers, and the public. Only later, when the jurisdictional issues were settled and the aid program became, comparatively speaking, an old-line government agency, did the unnatural relations between its public and its private parts begin to develop.

We cannot arrange for every program affected with the public interest to be controversial so as to keep it honest. The alternative is to make sure that the main considerations that affect the decision, and the people mainly involved in making it, are exposed to the public in an understandable way.

Here, too, we face, as often in public affairs, a dilemma. It is easy to say that all decision-making should be open to the general public. "Open covenants openly arrived at," said President Woodrow Wilson, but found that he could not follow his own rule and indeed consulted so little with Congress about his pet project, the League of Nations, that it failed of ratification in the United States Senate.

Radical groups on campus have been verbally Wilsonian—proposing decision procedures that provide a vote for whoever comes to the meeting, and then making sure the meeting goes on for so long that most of the moderate voters get hungry or sleepy and leave before the vote is taken. Open meetings of public boards and committees are also a perennial subject for editorial advocacy by the media. But every decision-making body develops some device for private discussion of differences among the people with the most responsibility. In a newspaper office it does not occur to the editor to open up to the public, with cameras and microphones and all, the daily sessions in which the editorial-page staff argues out what will be presented as the newspaper's editorial opinion the following day. Similarly, in governing boards (of regents, trustees, or directors), in regulatory commissions, in regular government departments, or in corporate executive suites, there must always be provision for talking out in private the most controversial issues, for compromise and face-saving and graceful backing down. If all boards were required by law to have all their meetings in public, that would just increase the frequency of lunches and dinners among their members, as they negotiate in informal caucus the positions they are going to take in the formal meetings.

A realistic policy of openness starts with the Public Executives themselves. Every Public Executive—in public or in "private" agency—might well ask himself several times a day, "Does this action of mine really have to be taken behind a curtain?" If its validity depends on its secrecy, there is at least a fifty-fifty chance that there is something wrong with the picture.

At a minimum, the Public Executives and the legislative

bodies from which they get authority and funds can arrange to discuss in public the major policy dilemmas with which the Public Executives are struggling from week to week. These cannot be kept secret anyway. They quickly become obvious to any reporter or citizen or public-interest lawyer who wants to probe behind the porous curtain of institutional privacy. Since the executives themselves have a stake in public understanding and consensus, they will often have an incentive to discuss with the affected publics the rationale for a move, and the alternative options considered and rejected, before rather than after a decision is taken.

In a horizontal society, where nobody is in charge and everybody is partly in charge, the "odd American notions" about countervailing power and plural initiative *can* work if
  • Several hundred thousand Public Executives, in private and paraprivate and public organizations, develop a personal definition of the public interest;
  • There exist enough independently organized ways of mobilizing the public outrage (the people who do the organizing will also be Public Executives by our definition); and
  • The processes of decision are open enough to permit representatives (including self-appointed representatives) of people-in-general to follow the play, recognize the players, and blow the whistle when they don't think the attitudes of the Public Executives are public enough.

A young professor named Woodrow Wilson recommended in 1887 that government administrators should "combine openness and vigor . . . with ready docility to all serious, well-sustained public criticism." It is still good advice—but it now applies to all men and women who carry public responsibility, whether or not they happen to be working for the government.

Chapter 9

Shapers of Values

The wayfarer, perceiving the pathway to truth, was struck with astonish-
ment. It was thickly grown with weeds. Ha, he said. I see that none has
passed here in a long time. Later he saw that each weed was a singular
knife. Well, he mumbled at last, doubtless there are other roads.

—*Stephen Crane*

As they explore their jungle of close decisions, openly arrived
at, the reflective men and women with the low-key manners
will discover new ethical burdens. The future executive will
not only have to guess at the public's purposes. He or she will
have to formulate and explicate them, too. As one of society's
style-setters, each Public Executive will need to develop a
personal sense of direction, together with a sense of personal
responsibility for the situation-as-a-whole.

From prehistoric times until the day before yesterday,
leadership in public affairs was exercised by a comparatively

121

small number of strong men. Their aim in contending for political power was a polity with themselves in charge. Once they were in power, the ultimate aims of organized society were established and announced from the top of a pyramid, which is to say by the strong men.

The more successful and affluent strong men collected as advisers the most intelligent subordinates they could find, to suggest where to go and how to get the followers to follow. These professional executives—sorcerers and generals, counselors and undersecretaries and business managers—hired out to the highest or most congenial bidder, or were pressed into service by force. They probably originated most of the policy that emanated from the top, but did not presume to be personally responsible for the goals of statecraft. Theirs was an ethic of manipulation, leaving to others the choice of direction and philosophy; the angle of their vision was that of a senior servant, civil or military. Down through history, the environment of hierarchy with its sharp distinction between policy and administration enabled the professional managers to finesse the ends and get on with the means. "Whate'er is best administer'd, is best." In half a couplet Pope captured a philosophy for administrators of all time—until our own time.

But if hierarchy no longer describes the way organizations work, if in complex industrial societies no person or small group can be effectively in general charge, the future executive will no longer be able to derive his sense of direction from "authorities." If he doesn't know where he is going, no one else will likely be able to tell him. Beyond the skills he needs to fit him for the game of forward movement by lateral consultation, beyond learning the specialized subject matter he is supposed to manage, the Public Executive (in public or "private" system) has to be his own policy-maker.

This would be a heavy burden even if the executive could concentrate on making policy for his own corner of complexity, and let poets and politicians worry about the situation-as-a-whole. But from now on each Public Executive has to carry on his conscience the knowledge that ("what with one thing always leading to another") his specialized actions or failures to act will affect the environment in which other men and women of action, in other fields of policy, will be wrestling with their own ethical dilemmas.

Each person with the knowledge and energy to act will therefore have some obligation to consider his personal contribution to the dangers that affect the ecosystem *as a whole*— the thoughtless extension of technology, imbalances that threaten to "run away to maximum," resource constraints that intensify racial discrimination, social tensions, and international conflict. No future executive will be free to act on the uncriticized premise that growth is good in itself. No manager of a technological process will be able to hide from himself the evidence that every technical advance has its dark side—unimaginatively destructive weaponry, the multiplication of threats to privacy and personality, the effects on human beings of urban life and work, the techniques for social control of the body, the mind, the fetus and the genes. Even the brighter potentials of complexity—beneficent control of the weather, of disease, of population, of nutrition, of mental stress, the elimination of poverty and large-scale war—can be realized only by Public Executives who are grappling with the situation-as-a-whole, not just one or a few of its parts.

Confronted with an urgent need for doctrine that covers the situation-as-a-whole, the American Public Executive might naturally turn to the basic documents of American democracy.

When in the last year of his Administration President Eisenhower appointed a Commission on National Goals, that well-informed group contracted for a hundred studies, held several long meetings, and concluded that it was hard to improve on the Declaration of Independence. When they came right down to it, those twentieth-century commissioners held these truths to be self-evident: that all Men are created equal, that they are endowed by the Creator with certain unalienable rights, that among these are Life, Liberty, and the Pursuit of Happiness—that to secure these rights, Governments are instituted among Men, deriving their just Powers from the Consent of the Governed.

Until recently most Americans were inclined to feel that, despite a residue of poverty and racial discrimination, these liberal doctrines were working out pretty well. They had provided both the motive power and the governor for our efforts to tame a continent, build a nation, and commence the construction of world order. They had encouraged and justified the scholarship that led to scientific invention and technological innovation—and to complexity's bright future. But each year it becomes more obvious that the institutions we have built and justified with these doctrines are not able to remain true to their purported purposes in an environment of accelerating complication. The purposes—equal rights, consent of the governed—are still incandescent. But our institutions— the uncounted thousands of units of government in America, the corporations and labor unions and foundations and universities and the rest—are sluggish in promoting equality and slovenly in governing by consent. They provide simplistic answers to complex questions, they give undue weight to precedent and discourage drastic shifts in direction, they treat the sum of specialized knowledge as general wisdom, they cushion mediocrity and build walls around innovation in the name of justice and humanity, they treat people as categories rather than as persons—and above all, they do not operate as though all our problems are connected with each other and therefore all the solutions have to be connected, too.

"If we are to retain any command at all over our own future," says John Gardner, "the ablest people we have in every field must give thought to the largest problems of the nation. . . . They don't have to be in government to do so. But they have to come out of the trenches of their own specialties and look at the whole battlefield."

It is not, as some would have it, the very size or complexity of social institutions that imperils our rights and threatens our integrity as individuals. It is the sluggishness of modern systems, as they grow, to recruit and train executives who find complexity congenial and can learn to swim around with confidence in uncharted ethical waters. Administrators who lack such confidence try to avoid detectable error by establishing formal rules and regulations, drawing too-clear lines of jurisdiction, and setting "objective" standards by which to judge human beings and their performance. Each becomes a thick braid of Lilliputian threads which combine to fetter giant institutions, reducing their receptivity to change and preventing them from dealing with people as individuals.

But the maintenance of individual freedom in a viable world order will require all large institutions to be receptive to changes, both in the people's expectations and in the technologies available to meet them. We have come into a new age with an old vocabulary, and the Public Executive has no more urgent personal assignment than to search for new, change-oriented ways of expressing the human wants and needs which are the reason for the executive function. And no man or woman who would lead can afford to feel that establishing the subjective human purpose of his or her own actions is someone else's job.

My own search began, typically I suppose, in my early thirties. Several of us, Washington civil servants playing small roles in the creative foreign policy of the Truman Administration, met every three or four weeks for an evening to ask ourselves and each other where we thought we were going. Our conclusion was basic, if unsurprising; it can serve our analysis by illustrating one Public Executive's notion of his internal moral gyroscope.

We should try, we concluded, to help the maximum numbers of people (not necessarily Americans, just people) to "maximize their morales" by fulfilling their basic needs. This required that we try to describe the basic needs of modern man. Then we had to define the reality around us, and analyze why it fell so short of fulfilling them. Then we tried to see ourselves as change agents, capable of bending the future toward their better satisfaction. In the oversimplified terms people often reserve for their most fundamental ideas, we saw man's basic needs as four:

• *A sense of welfare*—a minimum standard of "enough" in material living. How much is enough would of course vary from society to society and from time to time. But at any moment in any society there could exist a practical consensus on a minimum standard, by which Public Executives could be guided. Minimum wages, unemployment benefits, and legislative definitions of the poverty line are contemporary efforts to quantify "enough."

• *A sense of equity*—the individual's feeling that he or

she is being treated justly, not as measured by some ultimate or universal standard, but as compared with the treat-
ment accorded to other persons in comparable situations.

• *A sense of achievement*—the individual's feeling that
the group of which he or she is a part is making progress
in some generally accepted direction. For people in organized society, high morale seems to depend not so much on
what goals people choose as on their shared feeling of movement toward them.

• *A sense of participation* in deciding what those goals
will be. Modern man (of whichever sex) needs to feel that
he has some control over his own destiny and can influence
the basic decisions on which his welfare, equity, and achievement depend.

This enumeration of the needs of modern man assumed an
awareness by the individual of his interdependence with society. It implied that he cares about his destiny, and would
not passively accept what fate or the gods or foreign rulers or
his own family had provided in the way of environment. This
is of course a comparatively new state of mind for most of
mankind, dating in the West from the Renaissance and the
Reformation, spreading to the East through colonial governors, navies, armies, missionaries, traders, and reformist politicians, all of them from different motives stirring up ancient
societies by providing new wants to want and an exciting presumption of change.

Because the aspirations of so many for welfare-equity-
achievement-participation were (and still are) so far from
being fulfilled, I was never in doubt that my function as a
Public Executive—whether in foreign aid, magazine publish-
ing, political science, academic administration, international

organizations, American diplomacy, or university management—was to be an agent for accelerating change.

After a generation of accelerating change, I find this fragment of "moral science" still a reasonable guide to action in the 1970s—but what it means to me now is drastically different from what it meant then. In the late 1940s our perspective was heavily influenced by the experience of our generation and its perceived function in the public service. We had grown up amidst stories of a Great Depression, and had experienced a Great War. We were working professionally at European recovery and technical aid to the poorer countries in other continents. Business cycles, monopolistic competition, international economics, balance-of-payments analysis, and the revolution of rising expectations were our stock in trade. In our minds, therefore, the needs of modern man were all tinged with the economics of growth; and I was more inclined then than I would be now to set great store by their measurement. "Welfare" we saw as quantified in dollars and calories and square feet of living space. "Equity" focused on fairness in apportioning the good material things of life. "Achievement" implied an income ladder. The urge for "participation" was to be fulfilled in decision-making about economic status and opportunity.

As I tried over the years to use these concepts as a guide to action in other fields, they worked the way the United States Constitution works—old words acquired new meanings as they were applied to new situations. "Welfare" extended beyond the quantity of groceries to the quality of life. "Equity" picked up meanings in race relations and political arithmetic. "Achievement" was reinterpreted to include life styles in which success could not be measured in dollars or political power. "Participation" broadened out to include many kinds of community cooperation and international consultation not originally visible from the lower tiers of the Federal bureaucracy.

The setting of broad goals for future achievement is much more in vogue now than it was a generation ago. In the 1940s the fashion was detailed planning and rigorous control through line-item budgeting. In the 1970s, as we have seen in Chapter 2, growing complexity requires the modern executive to think of planning and decision-making as a continuous improvisation on a general sense of direction.

The executives who will do the improvising have an impressive array of new tools, chief among them the fast computer, with which to analyze options and measure effectiveness and cost. These tools will enable us to build models of alternative futures, choose with some degree of rationality among them, and work back from the most desirable outcomes to the most sensible actions in the here and now. But the key to the use of these tools is clarity about aims. In the most ambitious contemporary effort to build models of alternative futures, a Tokyo-based transnational research project called World Order Models, the researchers have settled on their own list of man's basic values: peace, welfare (including the concept of equity), and identity. It is not to be expected that every culture's short list of ultimate values will be the same, or that the lists will remain static over time. The important thing is that the Public Executives in every culture, and in every generation, try to make their values explicit—so that the means they choose can be compared in the open to the ends they profess.

The systematic study of the future has been compared to defensive driving: you try to anticipate the possible consequences of many judgments by others and yourself, and take immediate action accordingly. Man is, in Harold Lasswell's phrase, "a value-shaping and value-sharing being, interacting with his physical and biological environment." Man has now introduced technology as the central change factor in his environment and discovered that unlike Nature it does not regulate itself. He therefore has to regulate it by conscious management decisions. ". . . The problem of today," says an Australian anthropologist, "is how to use the intelligence of a relatively small number of men and women to devise ways in which patterns of behaviour, laid down in a million years, can be modified, tricked and twisted if necessary, to allow a tolerable human existence in a crowded world." The best of futures research, the part of it that may prove a major breakthrough in the administration of complexity, is not predictive; rather, it analyzes what might happen later to illuminate what should happen earlier. John McHale, author of *The Future of the Future,* says that at best the study of alternative futures can "set some bounds to danger and to hope," giving "a range of anxieties to the decision-makers" in order to sensitize them for the difficult choices which have to be made now or soon.

This approach to executive action—the study of futures as a guide to current policy—has come to be known as futuristics. Some of its more excitable prophets have concentrated on forecasting, and made their reputations with predictions of disaster if current trends continue. One danger in this approach is the likelihood of being wrong—economic growth may not continue at an exponential rate, population may be limited by chemicals and women's instincts, violence may not be correlated with population density. Another common error is to focus forecasts on some subjects and not others. In the physical world the use of some materials means they are used up. But in the future man's most important resource is likely to be information, which is not subject to the law of conservation of energy. Information feeds on itself, and multiplies more rapidly than rabbits.

But the most dangerous consequence of gloomy forecasting is that it may induce an attitude of hopelessness, a sense that things are so far gone that mere people can do nothing to stop Man's headlong rush toward the precipice. The extrapolation of present trends should not therefore be taken seriously as prediction. Its usefulness to the Public Executive is as a warning that our past had better not be prologue to our future.

A group of researchers at the Stanford Research Institute, trying to derive some educational guidelines from the exploration of forty "alternative futures," concluded that all these different kinds of troubles, present and prospective, are "surface manifestations of a pathogenic condition lying beneath the surface." They called the underlying condition the world macroproblem, and recommended to the United States Office of Education that conscious steps to educate Americans away from certain conventional premises would be an essential part of tackling it. I have adapted and added to the list of notions they thought should be derailed in the schools, to produce a list of a dozen premises every American Public Executive might well rethink, before acting on them again:

• The premise that the pride of families, the power of nations, and the survival of the human species all are to be furthered (as in the past) by population increase.

• The notion that knowledge has to be applied just because it is known—which leads, for example, to the conviction that if a weapon can be imagined it must be manufactured.

• The idea that the sum of expert testimonies is general wisdom.

• The tendency to adopt for the good of science a "reductionist view of man" (for example, the tendency in hospitals to refer to human beings as "clinical material").

• The premise that people are essentially separate, which enables us to suppress any sense of responsibility for the effects of present actions on remote individuals or future generations. (An old headline writer's adage makes this point with an equation: One million Asians dead of starvation = one hundred Californians swallowed up in an earthquake = one person murdered across town = one broken bone down the street = one fist-fight next door = one pinprick in your own finger.)

• The imagery of man as an economic animal, which leads to equating a society's success with its gross national product, income levels, consumption patterns, and the rate at which it uses up irreplaceable resources.

• The "work ethic" that treats the struggle for a better standard of living as life's central drive, and affluence as life's most prized achievement.

• The assumption that racial equality is best assured by trying to ignore racial differences, as in the liberal doctrine of racial integration.

• The belief that we can separate what we do at home from what we do abroad.

• The idea that it is safe for nations to be autonomus, that "defense" can be assured by "independent" nations.

• The proposition that democratic participation is assured by two-sidedness, parliamentary procedure, and voting.

• The premise, widely and sardonically accepted, that "what ought to be" is of course unattainable. And the consequent presumption that if something is wrong, it is somebody else's turn to fix it.

If some of our favorite premises are part of the world macroproblem, revising them will be part of the macrosolution. Whose assignment is it to unglue the conventional wisdom and paste up some new premises that might make life more livable and the world more survivable? The growing literature of futures research is reticent on responsibility; one reads that an unspecified "we" are going to have to rethink our goals, re-educate ourselves, revise our assumptions, ponder alternative futures, conceive new strategies, and take the consequent actions now. Who are "we"? It seems probable that basic premises, like "policy," will be mostly the product of consultation, clearance, and consent among the Public Executives in any given time and place. For the responsible executive, it's always his turn.

Is it unrealistic to suppose that each of a million American Public Executives, and the comparable executive leaders in other nations and in international agencies, can develop a personal philosophy that embraces the world macroproblem and implies a conscious choice among alternative futures for mankind? I do not think it is; executives do this anyway, even if they do not articulate their premises as philosophy. Each of us grows up with an outlook, a *Weltanschauung,* a policy for the future of the species which is implicit in the premises we accept and the assumptions on which we act. If our minds are capable of developing such an outlook, they are quite capable of *re*developing it. Not every executive will arrive at the same premises through study and experience; it will still be the nature of human cooperation that people can agree on the next steps to be taken without being able to agree on why they are agreeing. What the Public Executives can share in common is the experience of thinking hard about the world macroproblem.

In advocating his own retirement late in 1971, U Thant remarked that the next Secretary General of the United Nations should be "a globalist and a futurist." The same can be said of the men and women of the new Renaissance, whose task will be to retool the futurists' warnings into hopeful public action.

Chapter 10

Freedom in the Middle

There's no heavier burden than a great potential.
—*Charlie Brown*

In a household managed by people who can walk and talk, a baby begins to experience a sense of personal freedom when it masters the techniques of walking and talking. A fish which failed to master the art of swimming would doubtless feel frustrated in its life and work. Just so, in a society characterized by bigness and complexity it is those individuals who learn to get things done in organization systems who will have a rational basis for feeling free.

To the practicing executive, this proposition will seem self-evident. But the widespread inattention to the nature of modern organization has produced three illusions which have helped spread the curious idea that bigness and complexity are inherently oppressive.

The most old-fashioned of these three illusions is that things are being run by a very small number of shadowy bosses in a conscious conspiracy against the many. This doctrine is favored by extremists of the radical Left and the radical Right. Perhaps it betrays their own ambitions—the only society some revolutionaries can imagine is one in which an elite cadre composed of people like themselves holds a monopoly of effective power. The Right-wing illusion conjures up a conspiracy of liberal intellectuals, protecting a pot-smoking leadership of college students and Black Panthers. Left-wing imagery favors a small bipartisan business-dominated Establishment playing a Machiavellian shell game with the rest of society. Both images justify revolutionary activism. The healthy reaction is to confront the nearest administrative structure or set afire a symbol of power—the home of a civil rights leader or the headquarters of a bank, according to taste. But the conspiracy theory also helps justify revolutionary failure. Those who prophesy repression can easily bring it on.

The second illusion is that complexity is out of control; even the Establishment doesn't know what to do. The villains are not people but institutions. Things have become so hopelessly complicated that no one person can hope to make a difference. This view justifies copping out of personal responsibility for social outcomes. The individual is powerless, so there is no point in joining with others in social action. Better to seek surcease from complexity in a commune or campground, or even a campus, far from the crowd.

The contemporary prophet of powerlessness is Charles Reich, inventor of "Consciousness III" and author of a bestselling book, *The Greening of America*. Just as some campus radicals of the 1960s were allergic to power, so the adult philosopher of the youth culture is allergic to organization. The reason in both cases may be the same—they are suspicious of what they don't understand.

Professor Reich mixes with a perceptive cultural diagnosis a truly impressive ignorance of contemporary trends in human organization. He considers the "administrative state" essentially hierarchical, and seems not to have noticed the trend toward more looseness and pluralism in organization systems. "The corporate state has chosen to rely on hierarchical administration." "The random, the irrational and the alternative ways of doing things are banished." "Administration means a rejection of conflict as a desirable element in society." "Every person has a place in a table of organization, a vertical position in which he is subordinate to someone and superior to someone else. . . ." These old-fashioned administrative doctrines could not have been used as descriptions of reality by a person who had experimented with executive responsibility. It is hard to believe that a professor in the Law School of Yale University could be so sheltered from the realities of administration even on his own campus.

Uninhibited by exposure to the executive function, Reich correctly concludes that nobody is in charge, but neglects to observe that this means very large numbers of people are partly in charge: "The man at the top turns out to be a broker, a decider between limited alternatives, a mediator and arbitrator. And such a position tends to be utterly inconsistent with thought, reflection, or originality. . . . What looks like a man is only the representation of a man who does what the organization requires. He (or it) does not run the machine; he tends it."

From this detached-from-reality polemic, Reich derives a prescription for political and administrative inaction. Institutions are hopeless; the only hope is in a new life style which enables the adherents of "Consciousness III" to avoid personal exertions to improve their neighborhoods, their nation, or their world.

Resentment of the absurdities of bureaucracy and frustration with the complications involved in getting things done are perfectly healthy reactions. But the control of man's destiny rests in the hands of man as organizer. To deny his capacity to organize complexity is to condemn man himself, and that is too high a price for a best-seller.

A related reason for hopelessness is the notion that man can only be free *from* organizations, not within them. This is a recurring theme in political philosophy; many of us were exposed in school to Bertrand Russell's *Freedom Versus Organization,* and have dutifully shaken our heads at the plight of the Organization Man and the Man in the Gray Flannel Suit. In a *Saturday Review* article titled "The Jungle of Hugeness," Kenneth Boulding argued that things look bad for the individual in a world dominated by large-scale organizations, but cheerfully concluded that there is a good deal of room in the interstices *between* the behemoths, where "individualists . . . and people who positively like smallness of scale" can nevertheless survive. In the "Great Forest of society," the brontosaurus can do a lot of harm if he steps on you, but his feet do not take up much of the available acreage and there is plenty left over for the nimble and quick.

Yet we observe from day to day that people are able to work in and deal with very large organizations without suicidal frustration. In living-room seminars we pine for the corner

138

grocery, but a philosophical preference for smallness of scale does not keep us out of huge supermarkets. If you ask an adult what has been his most exciting, satisfying, edifying, or rewarding experience, you may find—as I found in asking this question of students in a continuing-education course on administration—that they usually had derived the greatest stimulation from associating with the biggest organization in their experience. The reason, I think, is that a very large organization has so many important decisions to be made that there are proportionately more, not less, authority and responsibility to go around. The larger the organization, the more lateral contacts it will have to make and maintain. As organizations grow, the number of "major decisions" about *internal* management may simply rise in arithmetic ratio to size, but the decisions about *external* relationships, the consent-building business that is in the broadest sense "political," seem to rise in geometric ratio.

In an organization system featuring horizontal relationships nearly everyone with the talent and inclination to lead finds a leadership role. Boulding concluded that "small organizations, even down to the level of the 'independent person,' will survive in the interstices between large-scale organizations." In our interdependent society one does not easily find the referent for the term "independent person"; but I suspect that those individuals will feel independent and self-confident who have learned how to survive and grow within large-scale organizations, not how to escape into the gaps between them.

One of the striking ironies of our time is that, just when we have to build bigger, more complicated "bundles of relations" to deal comprehensively with the human consequences of science and technology, many people are seized with the idea that large-scale organization is itself a Bad Thing. My thesis is the reverse: By the development of their administrative skills, and by coming squarely to terms with the moral requirements of executive leadership, individual men and women can preserve and extend their freedom.

Freedom is the power to choose, and the future executive will be making the most choices—whom to bring together in which organizations, to make what happen, in whose interpretation of the public interest. Those who relish that role will have every reason to feel free, not in the interstices but right in the middle of things.

Index

141

Index

142

Index

leadership: attitudes and qualities, 14–15, 24–25, 66–96
collective leadership, 13, 51, 54
specialists and experts, 70–72, 73, 125, 132
techniques of, 77, 79–82
see also decision-making; Establishment; ethical issues
legislatures: inquiries by, 112
responsibility and policy control, 33, 39–44, 56, 83
Lincoln, Abraham, 77
Lockheed Corporation, 58
Look magazine, 107

McHale, John, 130
McKeon, Sgt. Matthew C., 30, 31
McNamara, Robert, 28, 91
Madison, James, 41
man's basic needs, 126–27
Mao Tse-tung, 110
Marshall, George: Marshall Plan, 87
Martin, Edwin, 5–6
medical science and health, 9, 11, 29, 55, 123
Monnet, Jean, 87
Montaigne, Michel de, 91–92

Nader, Ralph, 51, 112–13
New York Times, 115–16
Nixon, Richard M.: Cambodia, invasion of, 21

optimism, need for, 131
by executives, 77, 85–88
organization systems, 13, 26–29, 32, 38, 46, 57, 138–39; see also business and industry; public/private relationships

Pentagon Papers, 19, 115, 116
planning see decision-making, planning
pollution see environment, decay and pollution
Pope, Alexander, 122
population growth, 9, 85, 123, 130, 131
Post Office, 52, 57

poverty, 124
war on, 37, 109, 123, 126
Priestley, Joseph, 9
privacy, protection of and threats to, 29, 109, 123
private philanthropy, 53–54, 60–61, 112
public, the: decision-making, power, and protests, 21, 31, 32–33, 37–38, 46, 47, 50–53, 68, 83, 109–13, 120, 127, 128
public/private relationships, 13–15, 32, 45–46, 48–62, 66, 100; see also business and industry; ethical issues; government

Rabelais, François, 70
Rapaport, Anatol, 27n.
racial equality, 51, 128, 132
discrimination and protests, 53, 109, 111, 124
RAND Corporation, 42, 58
Reece, B. Carroll, 53
Reeder, Gen. William, 22
Reich, Charles, 136–38
Reston, James, 116
Roosevelt, Franklin D., 77, 86–87
decision-making, 19
Rusk, Dean, 5, 20
Rules of Order, Robert's, 83, 84
Russell, Bertrand, 138

Saturday Evening Post, 115
Saturday Review, 138
science and technology, 7–11, 29, 57, 58, 68, 73, 123
and agriculture, 9, 11, 55, 56
decision-making affected by, 10–13
and medical science, 9, 11, 29, 55, 123
systems analysis, 27–28, 129
Schlesinger, Arthur, 5
Sisco, Joseph J., 5–6
Snead, Sam, 108
specialists and experts, 70–72, 73, 125, 132
Stanford Research Institute, 131
Stanton, Frank, 114

143

Index

72 73 74 75 10 9 8 7 6 5 4 3 2 1